99

THOUGHTS FOR

VOLUNTEERS

MAKING AN IMPACT RIGHT WHERE YOU ARE

DANETTE MATTY

99 Thoughts for Volunteers
Making an Impact Right Where You Are

© 2012 Danette Matty

group.com
simplyyouthministry.com

Credits
Author: Danette Matty
Executive Developer: Nadim Najm
Chief Creative Officer: Joani Schultz
Editor: Rob Cunningham
Cover Art and Production: Veronica Preston

ISBN 978-0-7644-9048-4

10 9 8 7 6 5 4 3 2 1   20 19 18 17 16 15 14 13 12

Printed in the United States of America.

Eric, my vanilla ice cream cone with a mustache:

Thanks for encouraging me in youth ministry and cheering me on when I kept volunteering.

Jeanne, Rick, Rod, and Bruce, some of the paid youth pastors I've served:

Thanks for investing in me as a leader and loving me as a person Over the years, by your words and actions, you've continued sending this message to volunteers like me: *"'You're not 'just a volunteer.' If you didn't do your job, I couldn't do mine."*

TABLE OF CONTENTS

Chapter 7—Full Circle: Leadership Development and Spiritual Maturity

Hi!

First, thank you for volunteering! Second, thanks for serving God by serving teenagers. I believe that no time ministering is ever a waste, especially to those under 20, even when we don't see the end results of our efforts. It's not that people over 20 are a lost cause; we're not! But with students, while you can't control all their choices, you get the idea that you at least have a shot at rerouting their wild energies and risk-taking propensities (Proverbs 7:7). You don't replace their parents, but because you're not Mom or Dad, you have this incredible opportunity to echo what great parents try to instill into their children. Even if you're barely out of your teens yourself, you can say things a loving parent should say and your words will carry more weight than you know.

Think about it: You don't have to be a paid youth pastor to be a caring adult with a powerful voice in the life of a teenager. What a privilege.

Whether you said yes to volunteer in your youth ministry in response to the call of God or the request of a desperate parent or leader, your "yes" has probably given you an emotional combo meal of excitement, fear, and purpose.

You might have joined an already thriving team of 15-20 leaders, serving a medium-to-large ministry in which you have one or two specific duties that allow you to excel. But if you're like many volunteers, you could be on the ground floor of a brand-new or rebirthed youth group. Or perhaps you've been recruited to maintain a sometimes-kicking, sometimes-napping youth ministry. In either of those scenarios, maybe it's up to you to do five or six things to keep the program running!

Depending on the size and dynamic of your church, you may be the only volunteer helping the main leader, or one of a handful of caring adults who just want to provide something for the two handfuls of teenagers in your church or local area.

And if your primary leader is new to this youth ministry adventure, you might feel like the blind following the blind! That reminds me of one Christmas break when all but two of us volunteers left town for the holidays—the others were all college students, including the youth pastor! Fellow volunteer Andrea and I led the youth service, taking turns doing announcements, leading the game, and speaking. We laughed later at how we swapped places during the night, running from the back to front of the small sanctuary—between the sound booth and stage—to support what the other was doing at any given moment. There were only eight kids that night, but we made it as fun and lively as if there were 30! We were pooped by the end—and glad when our vacationing co-leaders came back off break!

My volunteer journey began overseas in small military chapels. I was immature and emotionally messy, fresh out of a dysfunctional home and into the service (in 1980, this was the wisest thing I could've done with my 17-year-old life). I was stationed in Germany, just learning what responsibility and adulthood smelled like. But I had one foot in the world and one foot in chapel, smoking, drinking, clubbing, and incomplete without a man. Church leaders were happy to have attendance and someone willing to do something, so they didn't vet me too carefully. I think they mistook my sincerity for integrity.

Early in 1985, when big hair and shoulder pads were in, I was stationed at Offutt Air Force Base, just outside Omaha, Nebraska. I got involved in the large youth and young adult ministry of Jeanne Mayo, who has loved, trained, and coached thousands of teenagers and young leaders, many of whom now serve all over the world. Jeanne was and still is a leader-building machine. You can pick up all kinds of wisdom and practical knowledge from Jeanne's treasure chest of youth ministry experience at youthleaderscoach.com.

Jeanne's youth ministry was made up of over 450 junior high, senior high, college, and career young adults—a hodgepodge of people both military and civilian, all attending from the military base, the surrounding suburbs, and the inner city. Our core of about 70 volunteers gathered every week for a two-hour meeting that involved leadership training, soul care, and collaborative huddles within the respective age groups we led. Key learning revolved around developing intimacy with Jesus in our own lives, cultivating character, building healthy friendships, and helping others grow through mentoring and small groups—the things that remain relevant through cultural and technological paradigm shifts.

Jesus was captivating, and it was in this setting under Jeanne's mentoring and the dogged commitment of a small group leader that I haphazardly bumbled my way to a Christ-honoring life. As I matured in my personal relationship with Jesus, I grew as a leader.

Our team learned and lived spiritual and leadership reproduction. It was youth ministry utopia! OK, nothing's perfect, but it set a high bar for what the care and feeding of volunteers could look like. My husband, Eric, and I knew even then that we were part of a very special legacy.

Fast forward into the '90s, after the birth of our first baby, when scrunchies and flattops were all the rage. Eric and I moved to a rural city to help with a church plant. The first night of the youth ministry yielded 11 warm bodies—including four volunteers!

I was like wide-eyed Dorothy in *The Wizard of Oz*: "Toto, dude, I don't think we're in Kansas anymore." Welcome to real-world youth ministry, Danette. This second youth ministry experience, as I've learned through the years, was more typical than my first. This was a small church with a small budget (more like, what budget?), composed of a narrower demographic of teenagers, not the variety in the bigger community I'd just moved from. Yet in that tiny youth group (which grew by 100 percent within six months, I might add) in that Podunk town, we experienced life-on-life spiritual and relational growth, with no less enthusiasm. A changed life is a changed life, no matter where you are.

And I wouldn't change it. In 25 years, I've volunteered for several youth pastors of different ages and experiences, all with varying leadership styles. And I'm richer for it.

So in case you occasionally daydream of something different (read: bigger, better, and with more recognition), let me encourage you: You can have an alive and kicking youth ministry, regardless of size. You can be an effective volunteer, no matter what type of leader you're serving. And with God's help, you can make a difference in the lives of teenagers.

Jesus believes kids are worth it—not just the little ones (Matthew 19:14, Mark 9:37). Thank you for believing it, too.

I'm cheering you on!

d

INTRODUCTION

I'm not the main youth leader. I'm an unpaid volunteer in a helping role. A great "number two" or "lovely assistant." And I'm OK with that.

I don't have control over the budget, if there is one. I may or may not have a say in the infrastructure of our youth ministry. The buck doesn't stop with me; it just zips right by me. (I wouldn't mind a buck or two now and then.)

I still want to be equipped. I want to serve not only our students but also my lead youth minister. I don't have to be in charge, but I'm not a just-show-up type of leader. I want to be the kind of volunteer my youth pastor wishes they could pay (I won't argue, I promise).

There are plenty of resources for primary leaders—whether paid or unpaid—who recruit, develop, and lead volunteer youth workers. But there's not as much for those of us who are being recruited, developed, and led.

My goal in *99 Thoughts for Volunteers* is to encourage and equip the unpaid youth worker assisting the person leading student ministries. This is for the volunteers who, when they do their job, make it easier for the lead youth worker to do theirs.

Full disclosure: My goal is to build lifelong youth workers. Maybe you aren't called or inclined to serve God by serving teenagers beyond a specific season of life—and that's OK, because you'll still gain a lot from this book. But if you're one of those who are called to be a lifelong youth worker, may God use these 99 thoughts to keep you going through every season.

CHAPTER 1

WHO YOU ARE: PERSONAL CHARACTER AND SPIRITUAL GROWTH

PHILOSOPHY AND PERSONAL CARE AS A VOLUNTEER YOUTH WORKER

Volunteer...sponsor...lay leader...humble servant to the youth pastor...whatever you're called, it means the same thing: part-time hours, full-time passion...and no-time pay. But that passion squeezed between the hours and pay, plus your gift set, means you're an integral part of God's work in the lives of your students and the ministry you share with your youth pastor. Let's deflate the "just a volunteer" mentality attempt and inflate the truth of the primo skills and qualities that make for salary-worthy volunteers (even if it's just a pretend salary).

1: THANK YOU...WHETHER PEOPLE SAY IT OR NOT

You've answered the call of God, a desperate parent or pastor, or a combination thereof. You volunteered to help in youth ministry.

Thank you. You may not hear that as often as you deserve—not because people are ungrateful, but just because some people will be quietly appreciative that you're "doing your job."

Don't be discouraged when others seem to take you for granted. It could mean you're so good at this youth ministry thing that you make it look easy! And why overdo it on the thank-you notes when it comes so natural to you?

2 : PERFECT? NO. HUMBLE? YES

Do we have to be perfect to be youth leaders? That's a no-brainer: No.

But we should be humble, honest, and accountable.

Because of the privilege and authority God has given me, I give each of you this warning: Don't think you are better than you really are. Be honest in your evaluation of yourselves, measuring yourselves by the faith God has given us (Romans 12:3 NLT).

Humility will help you remain a good listener whenever a teenager is exercising critical spouting skills—I mean critical *thinking* skills—in the form of some diatribe about why cheating, pornography, or underage drinking shouldn't be a sin. Add a dose of self-control to keep your eyes from rolling too much.

Honesty gives you the ability to have nothing to hide. It's the sturdy bridge between humility and accountability.

Accountability to your youth pastor or a mature, trusted, same-gender friend will prevent hidden sin and self-denying hypocrisy. When you do come clean, your sin will be exposed and not exploded.

3 : SUPERSTARS NEED NOT APPLY

Bluefish TV put out a funny video about small group leaders called "Flaws of Biblical Proportions." A three-person selection panel asks famous biblical figures what qualifies them to be a small group leader. At first, smug candidates such as Moses, Samson, and David list their credentials. "Can't decide who gets the last brownie?" Solomon asks. "Cut it in two. Boom. Wisdom."

But when these model citizens begin to answer to charges of moral failures, their bumbling excuses are even more comical. "So I lied, I said my wife was my sister. They were gonna kill me," Abraham says as his eyes shift. "Why are we even getting into this?"

Finally, a regular Joe interviews for the position. He hasn't been to seminary, and he's not sure about his qualifications, but he loves God and wants to help people. The video's tagline is "God uses imperfect people."

As a volunteer, your ministry doesn't need a superstar or social worker. In time, your gifts will rise to the surface and you'll likely have opportunities to shine. But what your youth group really needs is for you to pick out one or two kids and connect with them. Call, text, or get together with them once a week. Show up at their games or concerts or whatever they're into.

That job description should be a relief for most of us. For all our talents, we're busy in many areas. Regardless of what other bells and whistles we ring, the bottom line is that we don't have to possess extraordinary oratory, musical, or athletic gifts in order to impact students and their families. Those things are the icing. Your quality time is the cake.

Want to know what Youth Ministry 101 is? A caring adult consistently involved in a teenager's life.

Boom. Wisdom.

4: EENY, MEENY, MINY, MOTIVES

What motivated you to volunteer in your youth ministry?

Some people volunteer because they want to be buds with the leader. And they'll dabble in

YM to check that block. But they really just like hanging out or learning from the main leader.

Others join a youth ministry team because they want to be a leader. They want to develop a specific skill or add to their leadership résumé, and youth ministry seems the best track for growth.

Some simply want to be part of a team, and their friends volunteer, so they might as well do it, too.

And then there are those—probably most people reading this book—who simply and genuinely love Jesus and teenagers. We get this unexplainable, motivated charge when we're around kids. We want God to use us to propel students forward in their faith journey. And we get refueled when we see that happen.

This may surprise you, but I don't think the other motives are bad. In fact, there's something good about each one. You may recognize a couple of them in you. But that last motive is what we should strive for, even if we keep a little of the other three. In all cases, if you genuinely believe in teenagers and want to help them grow spiritually, you'll likely dive in with more enthusiasm, last longer, and, consequently, become great at it.

All a man's ways seem innocent to him, but motives are weighed by the Lord (Proverbs 16:2).

5 : MOTIVES MATTER FOR THE LONG HAUL

Neither leader-motivated nor role-motivated volunteering is 100 percent wrong. But if you're in it for the long haul, remember that youth ministry is about youth. If you have a passion to influence this generation for Christ and are willing to pay attention to and develop relationships with them, God will help you do those things. Ask God to help you see and minister to teenagers as individual people more than as a demographic clump.

If you volunteer for a while and it turns out you don't want to serve teenagers, that's OK. Give your two weeks' notice to your youth leader, step down graciously, and give two big bags of money to the youth ministry.

If you do stay, do your best to serve from God's heart more than your own, and then you won't have to question your motives.

6 : WHEN IT COMES TO YOUR SPIRITUAL GROWTH, BE YOUR OWN BEST FRIEND

"God will always care more about you than he does your ministry."
—Jeanne Mayo[1]

One of our volunteers co-leads a men's basketball group every Monday night—really nice guy, responsible, shows up every week faithfully. He mentioned how great he thought it would be to lead a basketball group for teen guys. I agreed, and because I lead our youth group's "Connect Groups" ministry, I said it would be key to add a shepherding element to the group time, even something as simple as taking prayer requests at the end of the game. He stammered, "I guess I could do that. It's not really my strong suit." Because I value honesty over almost everything, I grinned and said, "Well, maybe this is your opportunity to step up in that department." He smiled and agreed.

Funny how important we realize spiritual growth is for students, but how easily we neglect it in our own lives. Self-leadership in spiritual growth is two-fold.

First—and you've probably heard or read this—you can't take people where you've never been. Others put it this way: You can't take people where you're not willing to go.

In his letter to Titus, Paul lists off a bunch of bullet-point teachings for this church leader to dole out to younger men. In the middle of the list, Paul says this: *In everything **set them an example** by doing what is good. In your teaching show integrity, seriousness* *and soundness of speech that cannot be condemned (Titus 2:7-8, emphasis added).*

You see, we teach what we know; we reproduce who we are.[2] So we can teach on spiritual growth with creativity and relevance, and we should. But in the most mysterious yet very real way, what happens in our private spiritual lives will rub off on those who follow us.

Second, we must never give ourselves permission to become spiritually shallow. Of all the shaping habits of our lives, I believe none is more transformative than time alone with God. It's a game-changer—more specifically, a mind and heart changer. For the sake of knowing Jesus, understanding God's will, and being led by God's Spirit, make time and focus to read God's Word and hear God's voice. Keep yourself in a position to be transformed by God.

The woman or man of God you are outside of youth ministry is more important than the role you play in youth ministry. As my fellow volunteer friend Kelsey says, "It's more important how you are when no one is around than how you act when all eyes are on you."

"Be careful not to practice your righteousness in front of others to be seen by them. If you do, you will have no reward from your Father in heaven" (Matthew 6:1).

CHAPTER 2

WHAT YOU SIGNED UP FOR: MORE THAN A RENT-A-COP

DIRTY WORK, TIME BUDGET, SELF-LEADERSHIP, AND LEADING FROM THE MIDDLE—IN OTHER WORDS, WHAT YOU ACTUALLY DO

No matter how experienced, savvy, and skilled you become with time, the behind-the-scenes dirty work still has to get done—set-up, teardown, powering up the computer, turning on the screen, and any number of other pre-service activities that make your youth group go.

Remember as you're doing these tasks that every practical and administrative detail contributes to a mostly smooth-running service and serves as the canvas for the big picture of helping your teenagers see, know, and follow Jesus. Whether you clean a toilet, set out snacks, or high-five kids as they come through the door, your servanthood *is* leadership, and it's critical to the mission.

7: LET'S SCRUB SOME TOILETS...NO, REALLY

"Whoever can be trusted with very little can also be trusted with much" (Luke 16:10).

My aforementioned mentor, Jeanne Mayo, used to tell us leaders this truth about servant-leadership: "If you're not willing to scrub toilets, you're not ready to be a leader." In fact, she once said that sometimes, when no one was around the church, she would clean a toilet, just to remind herself of what leadership was really about. The Jesus model reinforces the idea that servant-leadership trumps title, position, or kudos from others (John 13:1-17).

Let's be real, though: Some tasks are a pain. Before the start of my current youth group, I've watched and occasionally helped put up these curtain contraptions. I don't know who made them—someone who may now be in a witness protection program. But it takes two people to do this job, and it's time-consuming. The homemade curtains go on these rods that get fastened into stand-up poles that stick into heavy, metal bases. And if you don't bring a tool, you have to find one while your partner waits, standing on a chair or ladder. Did I mention they go up around the length of our sanctuary? It's not a hard job, just tedious. Not my favorite, can you tell?

But don't ever confuse menial with meaningless.

8: SHARE THE SCRUBBING

While there's a time to jump in and scrub a toilet because no one else is available, it shouldn't be left to you all the time. Whenever you can, delegate or at least share the scrubbing by inviting a teammate or student to help you.

If Jesus, who was fully God, was capable of doing it all alone but didn't, then you shouldn't either.

9: WHAT MATTERS MOST?

"My greatest fear is not that I will fail, but that I'll succeed at things that don't really matter."

Years ago I read that on the back of a church program and have had it taped to my brain ever since. Three of my favorite words, asked as a question or said as a statement, are these: "What matters most." There will always be a temptation to do it all, but as a volunteer with limited time and resources, you must decide what matters most in your ministry.

What does your lead youth pastor want most from your skills? How do you most want to use your gifts? That's a worthwhile conversation to have with yourself. (Just don't answer out loud in a crowded room.) In the meantime, the next two thoughts are meant to help you think through it further.

10: WWJD? MAYBE THIS, BUT NOT THAT OR THAT

What do volunteers do to help run a youth ministry? You could probably rattle off a dozen elements of your YM program. Here are some examples:

- Programming

- Small groups

- First one to arrive

- Sleeping

- Prayer

- Counseling

- Talk with parents

- Mission trips

- Follow-up calls

- Camp

- Sermon prep

- Last one to leave

- Drama team

- Teen drama

- Evangelism

- Campus Bible clubs

- Attending students' events

- Campus visits

- Worship

- Recruiting leaders

- Being your own secretary

- Date night

- Family time

- Conventions

- Book event speaker/band

- Fundraisers

- Ordering food for events and meetings

WHAT YOU SIGNED UP FOR

- Alone time (only in the bathroom)

- Reading YM books (see above)

Here's the thing: Everything on this list is good, useful, and important. Often you or someone else may suggest, "But what about this" or "We really should do that" or "Why aren't we doing [insert good, useful, and important activity here]?" It doesn't help to respond that you don't need it or that it isn't a good idea. But the truth is, you can't do it all. And you're wrong to try. (Highlight or underline those last two sentences, just to humor me.)

What would Jesus do? Great—the million-denarius question to load more guilt on you for not measuring up to the fully loaded YM program. But we had the answer from Jesus long before the bracelet was ever sold:

"Very truly, I tell you the truth, the Son can do nothing by himself; he can do only what he sees his Father doing, because whatever the Father does the Son also does. For the Father

loves the Son and shows him all he does"
(John 5:19-20).

If Jesus—fully God and fully man—was fully
capable of doing it all but didn't, do I really
need to finish this sentence?

Remind yourself, your teammates, and your
lead youth pastor that you know *you can't do
it all*, and you shouldn't try.

11: WHAT MATTERS NEXT?

One way to help you think about what matters
most in your youth ministry is to list your top
three priorities. These are not the top three
elements you think your whole youth ministry
should prioritize; that's up to your lead
youth worker (although you can always make
suggestions). Rather, from the list of youth
ministry areas given previously, which three
program elements do you believe (a) God
wants you to zero in on for this season and/or
(b) you're gifted and available to facilitate
or co-lead?

(1)

(2)

(3)

Now, put a star by the two in which you have
the most enthusiasm and margin to serve.
If you aren't already serving in one of those
areas, it may be time to have a chat with your
youth leader about it. (It's OK to talk out loud
this time.)

Why just three when there are so many other
things that need done? Because it's better
to do three things really well than to attempt
getting involved with a dozen areas in your
program.

12: BOUNDARIES ARE YOUR FRIENDS

Setting healthy boundaries isn't a new
concept, but when you enjoy serving, it's a
challenge to set and keep them. Throughout
this book, you'll read boundary-representing

thoughts that will add value to you and therefore, your ministry. Put an asterisk (*) by the boundaries you know you need to apply more often. Underline them if you're married. Draw a big arrow with a marker if you're a parent.[3]

13: TAKE YOUR BREAKS BEFORE YOU NEED THEM

Commitment = Good.
Over-commitment = Bad.
Burnout = Everyone loses.

Repeat after me: "It's OK to take a break."

Kelsey, whom I referred to earlier, serves in our church's college and youth ministries, both thriving programs. She's what I'd call an impact volunteer who brings her "A game" to every event. She also goes to college full time and works part time. "As someone who feels guilty way too easily for the littlest things," she told me, "it's hard for me to convince myself that it's OK to take a break."

It makes me sad to hear that from one of the most productive and high-capacity leaders I know. But the truth is, I used to feel the same way, and many volunteers do. We volunteer, after all! That means we show up because we want to. Why would we take a break?

The answer is simple: because you're better when you're "on" if you've taken time off. We all need downtime in order to be at our best psychologically, spiritually, and relationally.

I suggest taking at least one night off from serving every three months. Schedule it in advance so your youth pastor knows. As an interim student ministries director one year, I made this policy for myself and for our volunteer staff. I wanted each volunteer to be a whole person, not half.

And speaking of breaks, remember a weekly Sabbath. Don't argue with God on this one.

14: HOURLY SAGE

With your primary leader, set a predetermined number of evenings or hours you can commit to serve your youth ministry, and stick to that commitment at least three weeks out of the month. There will always be exceptions during high-intensity weeks with camp, special events, and other activities. But when you're a volunteer—especially if you work or go to college full time—you need to spend time wisely by putting in the hours you know you can be at your best and give generously, not begrudgingly and tiredly.

15: TO ATTEND OR NOT TO ATTEND

Go through the ministry calendar with your youth director and your spouse (if married). Determine which events you have the enthusiasm and time to attend, and which events you don't. If youth ministry is your primary volunteer activity, try to attend one or two student functions each semester. If you can't, be sure to follow up with the students and ask how the event went for them.

16: PLAN YOUR PRIORITIES

My pastor once told me, "You have to plan your priorities or they won't happen. That means if you want a date night, you put it on the calendar." The same goes for uninterrupted time alone with Jesus or one-on-one face time with close friends and with your children, if you're a parent. Make it non-negotiable.

Think about it: The kids in your youth ministry are so worth your investment of time and energy. But they will all eventually graduate and likely leave. Your relationships with Jesus and with family don't graduate. Invest in them on purpose.

17 : CHOOSE YOUR OWN BOUNDARY

Add your own boundary here:

Now you can say you contributed to this book...you're a co-author!

Seriously, there's probably something specific you know could pull you past the point of what's healthy. What is it? Write it on that line.

Tell a trusted friend what you wrote, and give that person permission to, as I might say to a friend, "get all up in your business" regarding this area of your life. Better yet, don't wait for your friend to ask. Regularly share that information and ask your friend to pray with you about it. Be willing to restructure your priorities in order to maintain wise and God-honoring boundaries.

CHAPTER 3

WHAT YOU MEAN TO THEM: KEY RELATIONSHIPS IN MINISTRY

WORKING WELL WITH TEENAGERS, PARENTS,
CHURCH LEADERS, AND THE REST OF
THE TEAM

I recently told a fellow volunteer, "I would love to recruit and develop volunteers who would do this no matter who the youth pastor is...just because they love teenagers." She agreed. I'll take a half-dozen dedicated adults over "just show up" warm bodies any day. Give me a handful of dedicated adults who "get it"—who understand that it *really* is all about the kids, and are willing to give a couple of hours a week directly to them, not just to the program—and we can make an impact!

Long after high school graduation, that's what students remember. Our bells and whistles, skits and games, pizza and pop all contribute to their youth group experience. But you and I are what they want and need in their lives—our attention, challenges, affirmation, prayers, and face time outside the program. Our consistent and Christ-like influence over time helps inform teenagers' faith development, choices, and their ability to reproduce authentic relationships with others.

Believe it or not, you're also influential in parents' lives—sometimes directly, sometimes only indirectly. Most parents notice and appreciate when other caring adults pay attention to their kids.

One day I was walking through the church lobby and, out of the window, saw a youth worker, Javin, playing catch across the lawn. As I walked by I realized the kid catching was my son. It was such a seemingly unspiritual picture. But no matter how many teenagers I've loved and invested in over the years, I can't tell you how much it meant to see this simple investment of time and attention in my own kid's life. Trust me, that's how other moms and dads feel when you and I connect with their children. It never gets old. It sends powerful messages: "You're not alone." "I've got your back." "I'm not you, but I'm for you and your child."

Parents may not thank you, but nearly all of them value your voice and presence in their teenagers' lives. It doesn't matter that you're not the paid youth pastor. What matters is that you give a rip about their kid.

WHAT YOU MEAN TO THEM

18: GIVE AWAY WHAT YOU WANT MOST

We all want others to reach out to us and make us feel important, to listen and really hear us, to push past our bad attitudes and verbal slipups ("What the *bleep* did you just say??"), and see beyond the masks we wear. And if other people initiate the conversation, that's even better.

But what happens when people aren't gutsy enough to push, see, or initiate? It's easy to retreat inward and write them off as selfish or cliquish. And while that's the case sometimes, more often than not, teenagers and adults alike are hiding behind their own masks, feeling trapped in their own insecurities and battling embarrassment from their own foot-in-mouth syndrome. ("Did I just say that out loud?! I hope no one posts that on Facebook®!").

So make the first gutsy move. Push past your insecurity or pride, as well as the other person's obstacles, and start the conversation. Be the kind of friend to adults and the

potential mentor to teenagers you wish
someone would be to you.

19: "GOOD TO GREAT" DIDN'T START WITH JIM COLLINS[4]

My friend Stephanie once said, "A good
volunteer knows youth ministry...a great
volunteer also understands the youth
minister." Do your youth minister a favor
and figure out his or her leadership style.
You don't need to be a clone or even agree
with your youth leader on everything. But
make yourself easy to work with by being
agreeable in your attitude and willing to follow
your youth pastor's leadership style without
compromising your own. One strategy for
doing this is to serve in a way you would want
to be served if you were in charge.

Examples from Ryan, a youth ministry
volunteer:

• Observe your youth pastor's weaknesses

and help minimize them.

- Know and understand your youth pastor's ministry vision.*

- Verbally support your leader and their vision even when they aren't in the room.

20: UNPAID SHOULD NOT EQUAL UNCOMMITTED

Treat your ministry with the respect and responsibility you would give your paid job. Unless you're still in the *my mom wakes me by shaking my foot* stage, you'd never be more than 10 minutes late for work or not show up for work without calling. Not being paid to do youth ministry shouldn't cheapen your commitment to it.

Volunteering doesn't mean you're on duty 24/7. But it does mean that for those times and events to which you have committed, you should come early—and if you're able, stay after most students have gone. If your youth group has pre-service prayer, be there, too.

Simply put, be the kind of volunteer your youth pastor wishes he or she could pay.

21: STEAL STUFF

It's important to learn to create devotionals and small group talks that are birthed out of your personal Bible study and God-times. But like all of us, there are weeks when you've got nothing.

When you need a break from writing your own curriculum, trust that the Holy Spirit has doled out good ideas to other people. It's OK to take their stuff and tailor it to your students. Pray over it as fervently as if you'd written it yourself, and God will help you add your own flavor to it.[5]

FEEDBACK FROM THE TRENCHES

WHAT YOU MEAN TO THEM

This next bundle of thoughts (22-29) was birthed from a workshop I've facilitated at the annual Simply Youth Ministry Conference.[6] One year, I tapped a bunch of youth pastors from all over the country and asked this simple question: What do youth pastors really want from their volunteers? Below are some of the most common answers.

22: BECOME AN OWNER

Take ownership of tasks. Don't wait for your youth pastor to give you directions on things you know would help. For example, when you know how the room needs to be set up and you show up early, bless your leader by starting the setup without being asked. Bonus use of time and energy: Ask a teenager to meet you at youth group early for this purpose and catch up on this student's life as you're moving chairs into place.

2 3 : BE RIGHT ON TIME

Being right on time isn't only about punctuality in volunteer world. When you are consistently prompt, that makes you reliable. It's a great indicator to your ministry director that you're dependable and can be trusted with greater responsibility. In your marketplace job or in your ministry, being on time is no small thing.

2 4 : BE RIGHT ON CUE

Along with being right on time, be predictable in your attitudes and behavior. I'm not talking about being exaggeratedly friendly 100 percent of the time. Being right on cue in your responses to others, no matter what's going on, means people don't have to tiptoe around you because you're moody or because when one person has upset you, you're going to snap at everyone else. You probably know people like that. You never know when they're going to be in a bad mood. And you can't tell until it's too late when they're going to overreact to something said. When they're having a good day, they're nice to be around. But when they're mad or depressed, everyone knows it—man, woman, teenager, and child. Even the dog hides.

We all require outlets for frustration, and we need the freedom to be honest with our key friends and leaders about tough stuff going on in our lives. But we also have to be mature enough to control negative responses and body language, especially around teenagers, who sometimes have a hard enough time controlling their own outbursts, without an adult setting a bad example.

Let a leader know before or after an event when you're emotionally vulnerable. Sometimes it helps just knowing that a teammate is aware. Don't make everyone suffer for it.

25: BRING IT

Bring energy with you! Whether it's your midweek service or your small group, don't leave it to your youth pastor to be a party on two legs that pumps everyone up. They need your energy and positive attitude as much as you need theirs. You don't need to be phony; just act excited about announcements, games, and your interactions with students. And if it's not in your personality to be excited, at least be upbeat. Students will feed off your positive attitude. So bring it!

26: GET OUT MORE. NO, REALLY: GET OUT

Connect with your students outside of church. Believe it or not, one hour a week of phone and face-to-face follow-up with one or two teenagers is worth as much or more than showing up for every main group event. Even if you only have one or two free nights in a month, you can choose one afternoon to meet a teenager for lunch, and another evening to attend a student's school event. Make a point of getting out of church world and occasionally showing up in a teenager's world.

"This is when it really becomes about the students and not about the youth group," says fellow volunteer Kelsey. "We all want our youth groups to succeed, but by spending time with students one on one, you're investing in a soul, not a program."

27: BALANCE RELATIONSHIPS AND PROGRAM

As a volunteer with limited hours, you may wrestle with how much time to put into your program versus investing in relationships with students. This can be a tough balance because some seasons or specific events will require your logistical or behind-the-scenes support. Think retreat or camp prep: Only youth workers realize how much stuff has to be ordered ahead of time, not to mention reserving vans and cabins and hotel rooms, and other key planning details—all of which can suck up a lot of time.

But don't kid yourself: Over the long haul, relationships won't thrive if you pour more into your program than into the people. For the health of your ministry life, the program needs to support your investment in people, not the other way around.

28: VALUE POTENTIAL OVER PERFECTION

Whether building people or programs, focus on potential, not perfection.

Imagine your teenagers on a scale from 0 to 10—0 being uninterested in knowing Jesus, 10 meaning full-on, flat-out committed to serving him for the rest of their lives. A score in the middle of that scale would represent someone who is growing in conviction, knowledge, and delight in Jesus. We all want our students to be at a 10, as well as ourselves! But focus on helping move teenagers from one point to the next on their spiritual journey.

If they're at 0, introduce them to the idea that Jesus is real and even worth following. If they're at 4, challenge them with baby steps that lead to regular spiritual disciplines such as daily time with God, Scripture reading, and telling friends what Jesus has done in their lives. If they're at 8, give them greater challenges such as regular fasting, Scripture memorization, and ministry responsibilities that help them develop as leaders.

My friend Joshua cringes at scale metaphors. He makes a great point when he says that it's not about "levels" and who's closest to God. "You're either growing, staying the same, or dying," Joshua said in a conversation "As long as we're all still growing, we're on the same level." This can be a helpful perspective with youth. Yes, with age we get wiser and know more than teenagers, but we're all still in process.

Scales and semantics notwithstanding, it's gratifying to see teenagers move along in their walk with God, even in little ways. You encourage their potential, and let God propel them toward maturity.

29: DON'T BE A "YES-PEEP"

Youth pastors don't need volunteers who go along with everything they say. They need a different perspective at times. If you've got another viewpoint, care enough about your youth pastor and the program to say it. Just be respectfully honest if you disagree with something. If your difference is about something fairly consequential, have a private conversation that can't be misinterpreted by others as disrespect on your part.

30: MENTOR A GROUP

You can't individually disciple every student, so choose two in whom you believe God wants you to invest or mentor. Meet with them twice a month (or more frequently if you have time). When you don't even have that margin in your schedule, group mentor three or more students at a time in a small group. It's better than not investing at all, or hit-and-miss connecting at your main youth service.

31: SEND GROUP TEXTS

To stay connected between group times, send a sincere message to a group of teenagers, a text that can apply to more than one student. They may not all text back, but most will know that you thought of them.

Examples:

- Hi. Thinking of you. How can I be praying for you this week?

- Hey, what's up?

- Hi. Are we going to see you this week/tonight? I hope so...it just won't be the same without you.

- What time are you getting here tonight? I want you to meet a new student.

- I'm gonna [insert activity*] this Saturday. Want to meet up?

[*That list could include hitting the mall, long

boarding, getting some guys/girls together to hang out, going to an appropriate movie, working out, going to your favorite brain-freezing yogurt shop or artery-clogging eatery.]

WHAT YOU MEAN TO THEM

CHAPTER 4

MUSH! LET YOUR INNER SLED DOG OFF THE HOOK

DOING WHAT YOU DO BEST WITHOUT FEELING INADEQUATE BECAUSE OF WHAT YOU DON'T DO SO WELL

The "Last Great Race on Earth"—otherwise known as The Iditarod Trail Sled Dog Race—combines danger, dogs, and about 1,000 miles of subfreezing temperatures in a competition on Alaskan terrain that's both extreme and breathtaking. You'd think a city kid like me wouldn't want to be anywhere near it, and you'd be right. But I like dogs, teamwork, and athleticism, so this sport fascinates me.

Beginning the first Saturday in March each year, the Iditarod pits upwards of 70 teams—each with 16 dogs and one human on an oversized double-bladed ice skate—that race from Anchorage to Nome.

So what does the Iditarod have to do with youth ministry volunteers?

Unless you've grown up in Alaska or, like me, you've developed an out-of-place, enamored interest in it, when you hear "Iditarod," you probably think of Siberian Huskies or Malamutes. And if you've seen movies like *Eight Below*, *Snow Dogs*, or *Balto*, that image is reinforced.

However, one of the most interesting facts about the Iditarod isn't the hazardous, snakelike course or the hundreds of pounds of gear on each sled. It's the fact that the best sled dog teams are formed from mixed breeds. In other words: mutts.

When I learned this interesting detail, I immediately made a connection to the youth ministry teams I've been part of. The application is relevant to leaders in general, really. I realize I sound like I'm comparing volunteers to pooches, but stick with me! As you'll see, this is just another take on the business axiom, "Get the right people on the bus." Check out this observation from now-deceased musher, Don Bowers:

> *Over the years, mushers have mixed all sorts of breeds in attempts to find the perfect sled dog. Some have been quite successful. Nowadays, when referring to sled dogs, most mushers don't talk about what breed they are, but from whose kennel and what lineage they descend,*

such as "That's a Buser dog," or "That one's from Diana Moroney's Ruby line." In short, the average Iditarod sled dog is basically a mutt—albeit a carefully bred and highly prized one.7

The fact that mutts become champion sled dogs made me think about how the most effective youth workers aren't always people that those outside of YM think of as "purebreds." You know the stereotype: 20-something, cool, musically gifted, and trendily dressed. Although people fitting that description are valued and needed, if they are the only type on a youth ministry team, the group isn't getting a socially or relationally well-balanced diet. Students will mature into the demographic that's discipling them!

In the dog-racing world, all-Husky teams are well respected. Yet professional mushers know that many of the best sled dogs are made of mutts. In the same way, incredible volunteer teams are simply a mixed bag of deeply committed and well-mentored people. Some may even have quirky personalities or be a little nerdy. Rather than insulting, that's good news for the *no-longer-cool* and *never-was-cool* among us!

It takes all types of people to disciple students. Whether cool or nerdy, band geek or surfer-dude, snack queen or game king (or vice versa), it doesn't matter. Teenagers simply need consistent and caring adults.

Just when I think I can build a better youth worker from a template, some outside-the-lines, unassuming volunteer becomes one of the most reliable, loved, and listened-to youth workers—a "mutt," if you will, who connects with kids in meaningful ways.

Remember this scruffy little tidbit next time you start comparing yourself with another breed of youth worker.

32: SLED DOGS AND YOUTH WORKERS

J.T. Bean was a youth pastor in Illinois for 17 years. He once shared a few observations with me after taking his son on a dog-mushing trip in Canada:

> *"The only time the dogs are barking is when the sled is anchored into the snow and ice." Secured in their harnesses, tied to the sled, and with the hook in the snow, they constantly tugged and barked, J.T. noticed.*

> *"All they want to do is run. That's what they're born to do. Once you release the anchor, off they go! The barking suddenly stops and it is the most peaceful and quiet experience. All you can hear is the wind, the sled gliding over the snow and ice, and the padding of the dogs' constantly churning paws.*

> *"Many times the people we lead complain. But perhaps that's because we're holding them back. Once we release them and let them run, they can do what they are born to do."*

If, at some point, you become a lead youth worker, keep J.T.'s words in mind as you recruit and develop your team.

In the meantime, using sled dogs as an analogy for volunteer youth workers, let's look at the strengths of each dog's role and compare these canines to leaders in the Bible—as well as those in a youth ministry.

3 3 : LEAD, SWING, TEAM, OR WHEEL?

Did you know that different dogs on a team have different roles? They are placed into specific positions relative to the sled harness and according to their personalities and strengths. They are *lead*, *swing*, *team*, or *wheel dogs*. Some dogs can run in more than one position, even during the same race.[8]

When it comes to a sled dog team, someone once told me that without each member, with each strength and place on the team, the dogs would just sit around the kennel, staring at each other, or looking at magazine pictures of purebreds!

For just as each of us has one body with many members, and these members do not all have the same function, so in Christ we, though many, form one body, and each member belongs to all the others (Romans 12:4-5).

Here's a snapshot of each role:

- *Lead* dogs follow the trail, guide through storms, and set the speed in a race. Qualities of a good lead dog are intelligence, initiative, common sense, and the ability to find a trail in bad conditions.

- *Swing* dogs are directly behind the leader. They send the leader's message to the back of the team, and set the pace. They swing the rest of the team behind them in curves on the trail.

- *Team* dogs are fast, have great stamina, and add power to the team.

- **Wheel** dogs are those nearest the sled and musher. They must have a relatively calm temperament so as not to be startled by the sled moving just behind them. Wheelers are the tough members—the "brutes" in the back with the strength and steadiness to bring the heavy sled around turns.

Clearly, each kind of dog is needed on the team. A race cannot be won with only strong dogs, or just fast ones, or even solely smart pooches. All these types of sled dogs are valuable. And the same goes for a healthy youth ministry team. Every type of leader is needed and helps make a good team great.

34: BIBLE HEROES AS SLED DOGS?

Who in the Bible fits into these roles? I ask this question whenever I talk to leaders about the correlation between the roles of sled dogs and youth workers. Below are some of their interpretations. Remember that some people from Scripture can fit into more than one role:

- *Lead* dog leaders: Jesus, Paul, Moses, and Deborah.

- *Swing* dog leaders: Joshua's training as a swing dog prepared him to eventually be a lead dog. Aaron, Peter, James, John, and John the Baptist also come to mind.

- *Team* dog leaders: Jonathan always stayed one step ahead of King Saul and remained committed to David. Luke was along for the journey with Paul and was a great help to him.

- *Wheel* dog leaders: King Josiah pushed the people of Israel back on pace again to where God wanted them to be. We don't hear a lot about Jesus' earthly father, Joseph, but his decision to stay with Mary provided the muscular turning point in history.

Can you think of a few others? Jot down their names:

35 : WHICH ONE ARE YOU?

Now consider the invaluable functions of your youth ministry team and think about which leaders, including you, fit into these roles.

Four veteran youth leaders—Lori, David, Chris, and J.T.—offered me their interpretations on each role equivalent. It struck me at first how each of these youth ministers had unique perspectives on the canine connection. But on second thought, it makes sense. While some of the same threads are sewn into all youth ministries, every ministry includes elements as different as each leader.

Your youth ministry's "personality" depends on a combination of your community's culture, church dynamics, leadership history, and current leadership style, among other things. So I hope the following interpretations not only remind you of your own crucial role, but also help you think of ways to communicate to your fellow volunteers how important their role is.

MUSH! LET YOUR INNER SLED DOG OFF THE HOOK

For Lori and Chris, the lead dog is the point person and the one who casts vision. In David's ministry, the lead dogs are "a select few who are close [and] not only looking out for the ministry but also looking out for me." They might be youth coordinators or part of the parent leadership team.

Exceptional swing dogs are "great encouragers," Lori says, "those that always have a word to share and are great [at welcoming] newcomers. They're willing to let others take charge."

The role of swing dogs reminds David of his reliable parent volunteers. He agrees with Lori, that they "want to be involved but not lead," and so they serve food, set up and clean up, and are part of the prayer team. They "work behind the scenes to make things go. They're usually willing to give back because others are pouring into their students."

Based on the larger, urban settings in which Chris served during a 15-year span, he sees the swing dog position as communication-centric. He said, "This is the responsibility of the administrator or coordinator," whether that person is volunteer, part time, or full time.

The life of the party who stays up all night at the lock-in—that's the consummate team dog, in Lori's estimation. This volunteer might even plan fundraisers. David thinks of new volunteers as being like team dogs because of their fresh energy and contagious excitement. "They need the pace-setting swing dogs near them so they don't burn out," he says. "But their enthusiasm for ministry is so fun to be around." Dave knows from experience that they may not be dependable forever. "But for at least a season, they're giving everything they have as a Sunday school teacher, small group leader, game leader, or lock-in counselor."

Who does the heavy lifting while Mr. or Ms. Team Spirit is having fun...possibly for only another six months? Not surprisingly, the back-of-the-pack wheel dog reminds David of longtime Sunday school teachers, the kind of folks "that have committed to the ministry no matter who or what happens."

Lori says wheel dog volunteers "go through thick or thin. When the bottom is falling out, they are still around to support." From a very different perspective, Chris thinks they're actually the big dogs of the church, elders and pastoral leadership. He says, "They are 'first' by being 'last.' Their role is to keep the youth ministry sled on the right track" by giving oversight to solving problems and setting policies.

The analogies are endless and by now, you've probably thought of your own. So what would you say are the top two roles you best fit in, and why? Would those who work closely with you agree? Make time this week to discuss it with a few of your teammates, and see what they say.

36: GROW IN YOUR ROLE

You're probably either one of a handful of volunteers, one of a couple of digits on the hand, or maybe the only finger. (As long as you're more of a thumbs-up than middle-finger kind of leader, we're good!) Count your blessings if it takes more than one hand to count the members of your team.

And if your youth group runs fewer than 25 students, you likely do several jobs. So in which of our analogous sled dog roles does God want you to most grow in? Are you willing? What do you have to learn or practice in order to grow in that role until someone who's a natural comes along and fills it?

StrengthsQuest[9] is a practical resource I take my Christ's Place Leadership College[10] students through during the fall semester. The book is pricey at $25, but it comes with a code to take a quiz that, when answered honestly, assesses your top five strengths, how you might practically apply them, and what you

MUSH! LET YOUR INNER SLED DOG OFF THE HOOK

have to watch out for with their corresponding pitfalls. It's not as exhaustive as some of the other personality or type tests available. Translation: Your brain won't leak out of your ears when either taking the test or reviewing the results. And it's not aggravatingly pidgeonhole-y.

37: RESPECT OTHER ROLES

If you are new to working alongside a variety of people with different personalities, perspectives, and work ethics, it can be intimidating. It's much easier to work with people who pretty much share the same experiences and think alike about most things. But if you'll patiently get to know your teammates and see past differing styles of leadership and communication, along with any annoying quirks, you'll work surprisingly well together.

It's that "one body, many parts" principle from Scripture:

Even so the body is not made up of one part but of many. Now if the foot should say, "Because I am not a hand, I do not belong to the body," it would not for that reason stop being part of the body. And if the ear should say, "Because I am not an eye, I do not belong to the body," it would not for that reason stop being part of the body. If the whole body were an eye, where would the sense of hearing be? If the whole body were an ear, where would the sense of smell be? But in fact God has placed the parts in the body, every one of them, just as he wanted them to be. If they were all one part, where would the body be? As it is, there are many parts, but one body (1 Corinthians 12:14-20).

Sometimes it's hard to appreciate other volunteers if you don't relate to or "click" with them. Still, if they're serving faithfully, respect their diligence. If they're loving and relating to kids and not putting them in headlocks as they come through the door, learn to value their abilities.

How about your fellow volunteers? Write their names here, along with the roles you think they best fill:

38: HELP OTHERS GROW IN THEIR ROLES

You thrive when you do what you do best. Others thrive when you help them do what they do best.

Strive to be the kind of person who not only values other leaders but also elevates and propels their talents. I hope you have people in your life who do the same for you!

For instance, a younger volunteer may not be as smooth with announcements as someone who's been doing it for a while, but if the kids in your ministry like the volunteer, they may pay more attention when that person gets up to talk about the next event on the calendar. Coach that leader a little, give them a short script, and turn them loose with a microphone. Encourage them the minute they step off stage.

It's the same with small group leadership: It's such a key role, but it's not one that requires a top-tier communicator. If your opinion holds any weight with other leaders, be sure to affirm those who have a good rapport with students. If they have a growing relationship with God and are available, cheer them on in small group ministry.

CHAPTER 5

YOU'RE NOT THE BOSS OF ME! OH WAIT, YES YOU ARE

WORKING WELL WITH THE PERSON IN CHARGE

Work willingly at whatever you do, as though you were working for the Lord rather than for people (Colossians 3:23 NLT).

Ultimately you serve Jesus. Secondly, you serve the youth leader and the team. Thirdly, you serve the students and their parents. While I've emphasized that you don't have to sell your soul to youth ministry, think of your service with destiny-mindedness. Commit to it with the kind of intentionality you saw—or wish you'd seen—from a youth leader when you were a teenager.

Obey your spiritual leaders, and do what they say. Their work is to watch over your souls, and they are accountable to God. Give them reason to do this with joy and not with sorrow. That would certainly not be for your benefit (Hebrews 13:17 NLT).

Along the same lines, your job as a volunteer is not to start a sub-community within the youth ministry. Don't circumvent your leader's vision in order to push your own dream forward. Find out what the youth pastor's vision is—it should line up with the vision of the lead pastor or organization head—and then, support that vision in the context of your strengths and availability.

From this platform, let's dive into some thoughts on how to work well your main leader.

39: BENEATH THE SHALLOWS

On an ego-stroking surface level, what keeps us doing this youth ministry thing may range from marking the "needed" box on our self-appeasement checklist to being the object of hero worship. Beneath the shallows, most of us genuinely want to affect young lives for Jesus. This isn't a steppingstone to a greater position, because we see no greater cause than God's exciting, rewarding, and sitcom-like call to love and disciple teenagers.

With that in mind, let's be at our best, so that we can echo the words Paul wrote: *I have fought the good fight, I have finished the race, and I have remained faithful (2 Timothy 4:7 NLT).* This same apostle said his life was worth nothing, *"unless I use it for finishing the work assigned me by the Lord Jesus—the work of telling others the Good News about the wonderful grace of God"* (Acts 20:24 NLT).

The question is, are you OK with the *how*, *where*, and *with whom* God has given you to do the work assigned to you? It's tempting to look at larger youth ministries, with more volunteers than yours, and think, "They must be led by leaders better than me, or maybe God just likes them better."

Maybe you're too rational to believe that tripe. But Satan will continually use your ego as a button to push whenever you're tempted to compare yourself or your ministry. And each time he tries, you decide whether that button is operational or not.

40: THE SHEPHERD VS. THE HIRED HAND

If you're OK with the *how*, *where*, and *with whom* God has given you to serve, then you can determine what kind of youth worker you're going to be. In an interview a few years ago, Rod Whitlock, student discipleship director for his denomination, talked about the difference between the shepherd and the hired hand.[11] It applies whether you're paid and in charge or a volunteer and in the helping role. "The shepherd mentality says, 'I'm going to disciple, train up, equip enable, encourage, and strengthen the students,' " Rod says. "The hired hand mentality is, 'I come in, do my service, I have my nice message, my polished worship, then I go off and do my other things until the next youth meeting.' "

Jesus' take on shepherds and hired hands in John 10 reminds us that true shepherding isn't about a person's position in the volunteer hierarchy:

"I am the good shepherd. The good shepherd lays down his life for the sheep. The hired hand is not the shepherd and does not own the sheep. So when he sees the wolf coming, he abandons the sheep and runs away. Then the wolf attacks the flock and scatters it. The man runs away because he is a hired hand and cares nothing for the sheep" (John 10:11-13).

It is an attitude that says, "I'm not backing off when kids either confound or challenge me. Neither will I run away when a parent gets mad at me. I care enough to stick around as long as the Holy Spirit compels me."

Rod believes this is a huge key with youth workers because, "you can have all the right programs, discipleship books, and *stuff* in place, but if you don't have a shepherd's heart or mentality, it's just another *thing*. That's harder to measure. It's a little more subjective. You can't really measure how much of a shepherd's heart you might have... or somebody else has. But you can see the fruit of that. And there's greater fruit from a shepherd's ministry than there is from a hired hand's ministry—maybe not initially, but in the long run."

The Three S's

You increase openness and trust with your youth pastor by regularly communicating the Three S's: your schedule, strengths, and struggles.

41: COMMUNICATE YOUR SCHEDULE

The first time I was asked to be on a bona fide, established leadership team, I could tell that it was a big deal to the small group leader who'd invited me. At the time I was enlisted on active duty in the U.S. Air Force, where I'd learned important disciplines like punctuality and having a good work ethic. So I'm a little embarrassed by this incident.

Sunday afternoon rolled around for my first leadership meeting. I don't remember details, but for some reason I blew it off without calling my small group leader. I don't know if I was just being lazy, didn't plan my day, or what, but I felt bad—just not bad enough to call my leader and let him know I wouldn't be there. Maybe I intended to avoid him and hoped he'd forget?

Well, there was no avoiding him indefinitely, and his memory wasn't lacking. The next time he saw me, he challenged me quietly and directly: "What would happen if you were late to your job in the Air Force, or you just didn't show up?" I stammered, "I'd get in trouble... probably written up."

"Well, Danette," he calmly responded (albeit while boring holes into my skull with his eyes), going on to say something like this: "It's an honor to be on this leadership team. We don't ask just anyone. We ask people we believe have the qualities of a good leader, who love God and have a solid relationship with him. So when you don't show up, it's disrespectful and says you don't hold it in the same honor. I know you're not getting paid, but I want you to treat this the way you would give a part-time job. That means, be on time. And if you can't make it, call me."

I've never forgotten that well-deserved scolding. It made me appreciate leadership and think of service to God with reverence, instead of as a hobby—or worse, something others should feel lucky I agreed to do.

Be proactive in telling your leader about upcoming vacations, that "dead week" before semester finals, the week of finals, or job commitments. There are few things more frustrating to a youth leader than being told at the last minute, "Hey, I'm not going to be there this week (or tonight)." Emergencies notwithstanding, if you have a consequential role in the agenda, your leader can barely hear the reason and, at that point, doesn't care. All your youth pastor knows is that someone will have to fill your role.

If you can replace yourself, at least then you've taken that task off your ministry leader's list before it has a chance to land. Your part and your presence at youth group matter. While no one can replace you because you're so awesome, someone else can at least do your part when you can't be there.

So communicate your schedule.

42: COMMUNICATE YOUR STRENGTHS

There's a tension that many Christ-followers face: the fine line between self-confidence and pride. Some people can't distinguish between the two and, as a result, don't break out of their self-abasement, falsely thinking that they're humble.

It's fascinating that while some people have a hard time admitting their faults, others feel they can never talk about their strengths. I realize the opposite is true as well—some people obsess over their faults or their strengths! Let's strive for honesty about both.

When it comes to letting God work in and through you, it's not bragging to share your strengths with your youth minister. God is wildly creative and has had so much fun giving you whatever gifts you have.

One of the ways you cultivate those gifts is by telling your youth pastor what you think your gifts are and asking questions like, "What are some ways my gifts and strengths can complement your leadership and line up with your vision for this ministry?"

So communicate your strengths.

43: COMMUNICATE YOUR STRUGGLES

One of the riskiest things we can do is lower our guard with other leaders and admit weaknesses. It's vulnerable and makes us feel, well, weak.

In the name of integrity and health—both emotional and spiritual—tell your student ministries director when you're going through a hard time or struggling with sin. If your leader isn't someone with whom you feel comfortable sharing details, just give the basic version. It will help your leader better shepherd and pray for you. No leader likes to be blindsided if things get out of control.

Sometimes I tell my lead pastor when I'm feeling overwhelmed or discouraged. I may not go into detail, but I assure him that I'm talking to a trusted friend or accountability partner

Your pastor can't read your mind and shouldn't have to. You can't go through fire alone, and you shouldn't have to.

So communicate your struggles.

44: ONE AT A TIME

You're brilliant, creative, and dependable! You may even have more experience than your primary youth leader. And you've got a TON of ideas because, as I mentioned earlier in this book, you're so awesome. If only your youth pastor would tap your genius for events, fundraisers, retreats, and small group activities!

But before you explode with innovation, consider the fact that your youth leader probably has access to similar concepts through magazines, peers, and the all-powerful Oz—I mean, Internet. Usually because of limited time, resources, and manpower, they can't use all those ideas, at least not at once. It would be overwhelming if they thought they had to.

So rather than overwhelm your leader with a spreadsheet of your awe-inspiring suggestions, offer *one* idea at a time.

This is especially hard for creatives. (We're all creative, but I'm talking about those for whom creativity comes naturally and regularly.) It's like a dog learning to "sit/stay" while its master holds the treat. You can see its rear quivering before their master says, "Come!" People who eat, breathe, sleep, and spit ideas every time they have a conversation can exhaust people who have the responsibility of implementing and managing those ideas.

So just suggest one idea at a time. And wait a month before offering another. Keep an "awesome idea" list and be patient.

When you bombard your leader with multiple proposals in one shot, you send an unspoken memo: "What you're doing isn't enough," or "You're not doing things well enough or fast enough." You may not mean any of that. But once again, remember that you're probably not the only volunteer in your ministry director's life offering awesomeness.

45: LET THE DEFENSE REST

Defend in public; challenge in private.

It's a policy that's easy to recall and recite, and it's key to mutual respect in friendships, marriage, workplaces, and ministry relationships. Even when you don't like the way the main leader does something, even when you disagree with a policy, even when you think your leader is plain wrong, and even if there's been a moral failure. You could replace "even" with "especially."

In these scenarios, your ultimate and prayerful goal isn't confrontation—it's understanding and restoration of relational integrity with God and each other. Therefore, in all cases, support your program when you're around other adults outside of the youth ministry. Speak highly of the leadership, activities, students, and vision to outsiders.

If you feel the need to question, challenge, or even rebuke, do it the way you'd want it done if the shoe were on the other foot (and for some of you reading, it's only a matter of time before it will be). Privately and respectfully ask for your leader's perspective on whatever decision or issue you're questioning. Then listen. Your leader may have reasoning you hadn't thought of, or motives that will make sense to you once you hear them out. But even if he or she doesn't, you'll honor God by honoring your leader.

With whatever honor or dishonor you "sow" into other leaders, you'll "reap" the same in your own leadership.

46: CRUSH GOSSIP

There are no good reasons to bad-mouth or question your youth minister's policies or character to anyone who isn't one of his or her fans. The only reason you might make those kinds of statements is if you're unloading to a trusted and mature leader for the purpose of processing your feelings because you plan on speaking with your youth pastor about it right away.

The reverse is just as critical: When people come to you with complaints and gossip about your pastor, crush it. Politely. Directly. Without apology. Crush gossip.

Ask the person, "Have you talked to her about your concerns?" If that person says yes, encourage him or her to revisit the conversation, but not unload on other people about it.

Say something like, "I appreciate that you think highly enough of me to share this; obviously, it's important to you. But because I'm not part of the problem or the solution, and because she's my friend as well as my director, I don't want to gossip about her."

Once, a fellow volunteer I'll call "Bob" had a theological disagreement with our youth pastor at the time, whom I'll name "Shane." I'll spare you all the details, but to clarify, it wasn't a salvation-centric matter or a basic tenet of faith, nor did it revolve around a moral issue. It boiled down to the way Pastor Shane communicated a specific biblical principle to his students.

Bob asked Shane about it over coffee one day. At the end of the conversation, they agreed to disagree. Weeks went by and Bob continued to volunteer without issue—until one evening when he showed up at a youth prayer meeting Pastor Shane facilitated. Shane, a few volunteers, and some students listened as Bob began sharing a few flattering comments about Shane. Without warning, Bob then pulled his "but" out of his mouth. (Did I just write that?)

Bob said "But..." and proceeded to tell the students how concerned he was about Shane's communication infraction and how misleading he felt it could be. The students were confused. The leaders were stunned. Shane was blindsided. He calmly told Bob how inappropriate this was and that the conversation was between the two of them.

To Bob's credit, he later contacted Pastor Shane and apologized for challenging him in front of students. *But.* Yup, he pulled his but out of his mouth again, to reiterate the feeling that Shane was leading kids off a cliff. *Oi.*

Bob pulled me into his dogmatic diatribe in a separate conversation, so I told him I understood his concerns and didn't begrudge his questioning of another leader. At the same time, with a tender heart and voice, I expressed disappointment at his obsession over this one point in light of our youth pastor's life of obvious integrity and solid reputation as a Christ-like man and mentor to students. "This is way more about you than it is about Shane, and you need to figure out why," I told Bob. He actually agreed.

In the course of our 45-minute heart-to-heart talk, I cautioned Bob that he was posturing himself as God's lovely assistant, bent on setting Shane straight. "God called," I told Bob. "He wants his job back."

Crush gossip when it happens.

47: PRAY FOR THEM

The leader of any department is under a certain amount of pressure to do and be all sorts of things—realistically expected or not. They're in their position because they responded to the call of God or a lead pastor. Either way, saying yes to the job painted a target on their back for the enemy of their soul. So pray for your primary youth leader the way you'd want to be prayed for if you were in their shoes: regularly and passionately.

48: THE ONLY GOOD SURPRISE IN MINISTRY IS A PARTY

Michelle, one of our faithful volunteers, was about to graduate from college and transition out of state. We had her come up front, share her plans, and say her formal goodbye. She did so, and then threw us all for a loop by announcing her engagement. Murmuring followed stunned silence. She had told our leadership just a few days earlier about a guy she'd been seeing long-distance.

Michelle was highly influential, especially with our girls. So while this should've been a joyful declaration met with applause, she received wide eyes and dropped jaws from teenagers and youth workers alike. Later, a couple of the girls wanted to know what made it OK for her to get engaged out of the blue to someone none of us had even laid eyes on. A couple of moms felt slightly betrayed by Michelle, who had echoed their God-honoring values when it came to romance and dating. Now this?

When I was a young adult, I would have said it was nobody's business that Michelle was dating someone and kept her engagement private until she was about to leave. That attitude was reflective of my desire to compartmentalize my life. I believed that keeping my personal life separate from ministry minimized damage control when I made mistakes and things got messy. But that attitude made hypocrisy easier to embrace. The more I hid small but questionable choices, the simpler it was to hide consequential sins.

Michelle was a young adult; certainly, getting engaged was no sin. But by not sharing this major milestone with the youth minister before sharing it publicly, Michelle sent mixed messages that left the team to do emotional mop-up with students and parents.

You can protect your youth pastor from being blindsided by big news by simply keeping that person in the loop on significant events in your life—and remember the Three S's (see Thoughts 41-43 for a recap).

49 : MY LEADER'S A JERK...OR NOT?

What if your youth pastor seems to have you tied in a harness? Maybe you feel like he or she doesn't appreciate your strengths. You offer ideas (one at a time, even!) and you make yourself available to help, but your youth leader doesn't take you up on them.

There could be a few reasons:

1. The youth pastor's upbringing or job training has created a strong internal sense of responsibility. The digital music player

inside her brain is set to repeat the track that says, "If I want it done right, I have to do it myself."

2. He has a big ego, which leads him to do almost everything himself—in which case, the digital music player inside *his* brain is set to repeat, "If I want the credit, I have to do it myself."

3. She is so used to working solo that she's never had to or thought to ask for help.

4. I know one youth pastor who feels guilty for asking already overcommitted volunteers to do yet one more thing. So when he asks, it comes out ambiguously: "If anyone wants to [fill in the blank], let me know…"

5. This team-leading thing is new, and she doesn't know how to ask.

6. He's a jerk. Probably not, but when you think it, sometimes it feels good to say it. (Just don't say it when people are around.)

7. She may feel external pressure from a pastor or parent to do more or to be seen as the obvious leader. I knew a worship leader who felt guilty for taking a weekend off once in a while. She couldn't fathom training someone else to lead worship now and then, for fear of accusations that she wasn't "doing what they paid her for." Your paid leader may feel similar pressure.

8. He thinks you're incompetent. That doesn't mean you are, but if he hasn't experienced you being consistently faithful or helpful, he may feel you're not ready for more responsibility.

9. Intentionally or not, you somehow come off as territorial. It may not be accurate, but if you've given off vibes that you *have to* be in charge of a certain area, or that you believe you can do it better than anyone (even if that's true), then you need to back up and work on your character and humility before offering to take on more duties.

10. The youth ministry is under-resourced, and your ministry director doesn't feel she can afford what you need for whatever it is you'd like to do.

11. He likes you, but doesn't think you're the right person for what you're asking to spearhead.

For whatever reason, there will be seasons and scenarios when you don't feel overly appreciated. Maybe you played a big part in a small youth ministry but you've moved to a larger ministry where you now have a smaller role. That requires an adjustment.

But all of this misses the point. Whatever reason your ministry director doesn't use you in the way you want is secondary to how you handle it. Your heart attitude may very well be a catalyst to the opportunities God orchestrates for your leadership.

Keep the lines of communication open with your leader. You can continue to offer your help in certain areas without nagging. Or you can serve however you're allowed and give it three months to see if anything changes in your perspective or your youth pastor's perspective.

Keep a humble and prayerful attitude about your role.

Recommend ideas for specific skills in which you'd like to be challenged and ways you'd like to contribute. Ask your ministry director if there's something you can do to grow in your strengths or character. Be open to maturing in any area where you've been challenged. Maybe you're not ready to lead a small group right now. But if you're willing to read, develop conversational skills, and work under a veteran small group leader, you may be ready in a few months.

BE A SHEEPDOG FOR YOUR SHEPHERD

50: SHEEPDOGS ARE THE SHEPHERD'S BEST FRIENDS

Here I go again with the pooch analogies! Don't judge.

The other comparison to volunteers you may have heard besides the hired hand is that of a sheepdog.

"It is obvious really that a well-trained working sheepdog is the shepherd's best friend. Cutting his workload and saving time and money. These dogs don't see what they do as work!" So say the folks at the UK's allaboutsheepdogs.com.

What exactly does a sheepdog do that can teach us how to be better volunteers and offer stronger support to the student ministry director?

"In the world of shepherding a good working sheepdog can think for itself—sizing up a situation and acting upon it…often before the shepherd has even become aware of a problem. What's more, the dog has the welfare of the sheep in mind just as much as the shepherd. He is protecting and managing them for you." [12]

1. Our main youth leader doesn't expect us to be her robots or clones. She expects us to be thoughtful and smart in our helping role.

2. When you see two students racing up the pipes on either corner of the building to see who can reach the roof first, it's safe to size up the situation and act on it. To clarify: This is one of those rare instances when yelling like a crazy person is completely appropriate.

3. There are few values greater to a lead youth worker than knowing that his volunteers

take ownership of the ministry. When you look out for the welfare of students and the program itself, you give your youth pastor the security of knowing he isn't in it alone and that you're one of those volunteers who will do the right thing, no matter who's in charge. That's gold.

51: SHEEPDOGS DON'T BITE THE SHEEP

A sheepdog doesn't attack the sheep, although it may nip at their ankles to lead them in the direction of the shepherd. One herder wrote, "Our dogs don't bite our sheep, they are trained not to. A dog that bites sheep will not be trusted and is unsuitable." [13]

There will always be a need for nondefensive, corrective discipline in youth ministry. But you don't have to be a jerk to do it effectively. Private conversations that begin and end with clear expectations and assurance of your caring will go further than barking or snapping at students.

Two extremely useful books for learning to interact with kids in challenging situations are:

- *Boundaries With Teens: When to Say Yes, How to Say No* by Dr. John Townsend (Zondervan 2006)

- *When Church Kids Go Bad: How to Love and Work with Rude, Obnoxious, and Apathetic Students* by Les Christie (Zondervan/Youth Specialties 2008)

52: LIKABILITY, TEACHABILITY, AND FLEXIBILITY

Sheepdogs are known for being intelligent, playful, trainable, and willing to please. You're probably strongest in one or two of those areas. Nobody's perfect. I once heard pastor and leadership brainiac Rod Loy speak at a retreat, where he mentioned three key qualities that add value to any staff: likability, teachability, and flexibility.

You can be likable but so full of yourself you're unable to hear correction. And you can be teachable and willing to learn, but so bent on tasks that you communicate to people that you care about them, much less like them. And of course, you can be available and able to roll with changes, but if you're not a pleasant person to be around, you morph into a martyr, and if that rubs off on others, it poisons the team.

If you're not already headed in this direction, with God's help, grow into the kind of volunteer your youth leader knows will have a great attitude, is willing to self-educate and be coached, and can change directions without hyperventilating.

CHAPTER 6

VOLUNTEERING THROUGH THE AGES...ER, STAGES

SERVING IN YM THROUGH THE SEASONS OF LIFE--
SINGLE, MARRIED, WITH KIDS OF ALL AGES,
AND EMPTY NEST

Looking back, it's wild to think that I've volunteered with teenagers and young adults since I was a single emerging adult myself, and then as a young married. After we had children, Eric and I continued to lead small groups of young adult and young marrieds while, with his encouragement, I kept volunteering as a youth leader. And when our kids entered middle school, I asked them how they felt about me staying in the youth group, held my breath, and sighed relief when they gave me the OK.

As I write this, Ariana, our older child, has been in college for a few years, and Denver, our younger, graduated from high school in 2012. I'm now looking at ministry without children in the youth program. And I just signed my commitment card for the fall. I smiled when I typed those words.

Here are some thoughts from my own experience and from that of other youth workers in each age and stage. I hope these thoughts give you perspective, reveal a few helpful tips, and show you that no matter what life stage you're in, you can influence teenagers for Christ. They will continue to be worth the effort.

SINGLE IN YM

53: TIME WILL TELL

As a single, you may have more time than the married-with-children volunteer. Still, you ought to budget your time just as you budget money. It's been said that whatever time management habits you apply when single won't magically transform when you're married.

So decide on one or two time slots a week you can give to mentoring a teenager or leading a 90-minute small group. Be faithful to those commitments. That doesn't mean you should light the candle at both ends; eventually you'll run out of wax and burn out.

54: FAMILY TIES

If you like your family and they live within driving distance, visit them once a week. If not, adopt yourself into a family that would enjoy your company—think grandparents and empty nesters who like to cook!

Now and then, you need to eat food that doesn't come out of a box—plus, it's emotionally healthy for you to hang around people in a healthy marriage or family. This is especially important if you're like me and you didn't grow up Catholic or Protestant; you grew up dysfunctional. Being around reasonably healthy people has a restorative effect and helps you learn so much about what's appropriate in the way of communication, boundaries, and love.

Take mental notes and file them away for future use.

5 5 : INNER-CIRCLE FRIENDS

"Show me your friends and I'll show you your future."

"You get like the people you hang around with."

For years, we youth leaders have made these kinds of statements about friends to our students. We are not exempt from the underlying truth behind those sayings.

If you have a friend who knows you fully yet loves you anyway, and who points you to Jesus in big and little ways, get together with that person at least once a week. If you have more than one friend like that, consider yourself extremely blessed.

5 6 : OUTER-CIRCLE FRIENDS

There's something refreshing about hanging around people now and then who are in no way connected to your youth ministry. In fact, they may go to another church or even be part of a—gasp!—different denomination. My email signature has for years read "Same Team," because the muscle of our mutual faith is so much more powerful than any differences in our worship styles.

Building friendships with people outside your usual circle, who have similar core values but completely different interests, is one of the most enriching things you can do.

57: GET OVER THE INFLUENCE

People who are negative, extremely cynical (without being balanced), lacking in boundaries, or are critical of those around them are people you shouldn't allow to influence you. I'm not saying never connect with them, but people who bring you down just by hanging around you don't deserve a big chunk of your time.

I'm not talking about an "us vs. them" attitude some Christians have toward non-Christians. No matter how spiritually mature you are, if a negative, life-sucking person is regularly close to you, that person will eventually rub off on you in a bad way. And it'll show up in any given part of your life, including your interaction with teenagers.

You can love those joy-sapping people, and you don't have to ditch them altogether, but don't give them too much of yourself to them or take on their attitudes. Your time is too valuable to waste, so don't.

58: WHEN BEING ALONE PUTS YOU IN GOOD COMPANY

Learn to enjoy your own company by making sure your alone time refuels you rather than drains you. One way to do that is to keep in moderation media habits that have the potential of robbing you of time and brain cells.

How many hours do you spend watching TV? gaming? fruitlessly surfing the Internet? Don't hold your breath waiting for me to tell you to quit those things. Just think and pray about a time budget for them. Look at your week and decide how much time you can give to those activities without compromising time alone being restful, productive, and/or spiritually tuned in to God.

Consider a fast—for even a part of a day— from one or more media options. For example, allow yourself to spend time on social media sites in the afternoons but not first thing in the morning or late at night.

59: INVISIBLE T-SHIRT, PART 1

You're not dating but you want to be. Nothing wrong with that desire—unless that's all you talk about with your friends or in your social media updates.

Once again, in a mentor role, you have this prize opportunity to show teenagers what it looks like to live as an unmarried adult. Think of yourself as wearing an invisible T-shirt that reads: *This is what it looks like to be single and content (or, gulp, not).*

That doesn't mean not talking about what you want in a future mate or never acknowledging that you think someone's attractive (try to avoid "hot"—it's so 2009). What it means is being fully present with people, engaged in life, and continually learning new things, including learning to be happy with yourself (HUGE prerequisite to being happy with someone else).

My daughter, Ariana, grew up in youth ministry and had wonderful female mentors, single and married. She observes, "If you're good at being single, the kids who look up to you aren't going to be so eager to conform to a culture that says being in a relationship is everything. This culture doesn't have very many templates for godly single people, so when you are one, that gives teenagers an example to follow."

VOLUNTEERING THROUGH THE AGES...ER, STAGES

Married, single, or dating, a thriving soul is one who falls in love with Jesus on a regular basis and shows people what that looks like. Ariana added, "If teenagers see that you consider singleness as a gift, which it is, then they'll be more open to believing that as well."

60: HAVE MORE FUN THAN YOU CAN STAND

For all my pearls of wisdom on time budgeting and boundaries and balance—blah, blah, blah—I have a confession to make: When Eric and I look back on our young adult years as singles, singles dating each other, and young marrieds without children, we have great memories. We could stay out late with people in our small group, talking or toilet-papering people's houses and cars. We knew we would have the young adult energy to make it through work the next day. We could more often than not (and certainly more than when we began a family) spontaneously drop what we were doing to get together with others.

We had more time and energy, though not necessarily money. But what income we had wasn't going to major expenditures, such as roof repairs or saving for a child's wedding. It's not that we were irresponsible; we were just more available. We had a blast with our youth and young adult ministry! God used those times to form us and used us to help grow others.

Would we do some things differently? Sure, wouldn't we all? But enjoy your single days in ministry for everything they're worth. Allow yourself more time alone with Jesus to hear his heart and know his voice—before life multiplies the sweet voices of a spouse and children in your life. That will be a treasured time in your life. But don't fool yourself into thinking that this season of your life is merely prep for "then."

Grow. Hunger for Jesus. Enjoy him, people, and yourself. Have more fun than you can stand!

VOLUNTEERING THROUGH THE AGES...ER, STAGES

SINGLE AND DATING IN YM

61: YOU AND POOKY SITTING IN A TREE, K-I-S-S-I-N-G!

Sorry, I've been hanging around middle schoolers for a few years now.

So you like this person, or maybe you're already in a dating relationship. How might that blend with youth ministry?

As mentioned earlier, keep your student ministries director in the loop. As a volunteer on their team, your life choices affect others. Keep your leader up to speed on the progress of your relationship and be accountable with your conduct therein—not only your physical boundaries but also the way you treat one another. It all matters, whether your boyfriend/girlfriend is a youth worker or not.

For example, have you crossed the line in physical boundaries in the middle of the teaching series on purity? You probably ought to ask your youth pastor or another trusted leader to help keep you accountable and pray with you.

Did you two have a big fight right before youth group? It may affect your mood and the way you respond to people. Let a fellow volunteer or your ministry leader know.

Does your boyfriend think you spend way too much time with these kids and not enough with him? Does your girlfriend get frustrated that you want to play basketball every Saturday with guys in the youth group?

Even logistical issues come into play: Will your significant other's company dinner trump the fall youth retreat? Are you building your relationship totally around youth ministry events? Do you feel you can have a mind of your own when it comes to YM philosophy? Are you comfortable about speaking up and sharing your opinion on planning?

Two of the most effective dating youth ministry couples I know have made a point of not showing an overload of physical affection or goo-goo eyes with each other when they're in their small group or at a youth event. You wouldn't know they're dating unless you knew them. They're committed to being fully engaged in the program and, more importantly, the teenagers who show up.

62: INVISIBLE T-SHIRT, PART 2

Whatever the dynamics of your relationship, the invisible T-shirt you're wearing in front of others, especially your students, reads: *This is how you date.*

You're setting an example of what a dating relationship looks and sounds like. The way you treat your romantic interest tells everyone what value you place on that person. What an awesome chance to tell people why. ("They're a treasure in God's eyes, and I want to reinforce that by the way I talk to and about them.")

As a leader, you don't have the luxury of compartmentalizing your life or not caring what others think. Do you speak disrespectfully to your boyfriend/girlfriend? Do you flirt (one young adult I know calls flirting "unintelligent humor") or make comments that provide too much information? Simply put, do you talk to your significant other in a way that you want to see your students communicate in their relationships? If you're dating, what does your invisible T-shirt read?

MARRIED IN YM

6 3 : FLIRT FOREVER

I sometimes joke that if you need deep and sound wisdom on marriage, ask my husband. If you want shallow but effective ideas, talk with me. My No. 1 piece of advice is simple: Flirt forever.

Even if you weren't a flirtatious single—and it's OK if you weren't—now that you're married, game on! Saying things to your spouse that would have been inappropriate when you were single and saying them just loud enough for only your spouse to hear is part of the fun. (It's especially entertaining in the middle of the church lobby. OK, maybe I just like to see my sweet man's eyes get round as I say something and then go skipping into the sanctuary.) Whether by text, phone, or in person, don't stop being playful and romantic with each other.

I'm not suggesting putting on a show of ogling and groping each other in front of others. You or your spouse may not be comfortable with showing a lot of affection in public. That's OK as long as you don't stiffen like a board when your spouse reaches for your hand or gives you a little smooch while people happen to be watching.

However, teenagers and young adults need to see examples, and not just of stoically committed marriages. Dogged commitment is important. But sadly, some couples stay together solely because of their children, codependency, or a financial mess that would bury them if they split.

Let youth see not only your God-honoring commitment to one another, but also healthy romance in real life. Show them that marriage doesn't have to submerge joy and laughter between two people.

64: DUMB OR STILL DATING?

One of the dumbest things I see married people do is actually what they don't do, and that's to keep dating. They settle into existence, and a busy one at that.

Try to get out of your home once a week—even once a month—and into a neutral environment, such as a park to walk in, a restaurant, or a coffee shop. Flirt, talk, argue, catch up, or walk quietly hand in hand. Just be together.

If dating your spouse isn't a priority when you're first married, it's only going to be more challenging with children in the mix. Even a cheap date that leaves you feeling connected is better than no date and no connection.

Side note: Updating social media during your date to proclaim that you're on a date...lame! Do it before or after your date, if you must (not a bad example to set, I admit). But during your time together, put your phone away. (Don't make me show up and regulate!)

65: INVISIBLE T-SHIRT, PART 3

Beyond commitment and healthy interaction, if you're married, what does your invisible T-shirt read? I think that's simple: *Here's what marriage looks like.*

Lynna had been in my youth group as a teenager and later interned for another youth ministry. Once she confided how frustrating it was to watch her youth pastor and her husband, who was also the worship leader for the youth group. They would argue in front of students about any number of things logistical, philosophical. And when they argued, things got heated in their facial expressions and voice tones.

The health of your marriage has to come first, and everyone around you should know that's your priority. You're going to have arguments, but try to keep them private. If you disagree in public, fight fair. No name-calling, sarcasm, or condescension. Maintain a respectful attitude in your voice and body language.

Whenever you can do so in conversations, written communication, or public speaking, without sounding scripted, use the language of, "My husband/wife and I...." Make a point of including your spouse in your decisions and letting everyone know that even if they aren't able to volunteer with you, you two are a team.

Especially if your spouse doesn't serve in youth ministry with you, be sure to talk them up when they aren't around and to talk up to them when they are. You don't have to go overboard about how "hot" they are (are we over that yet?) or how they're the "best in the world." (I'm not a big fan of the "could apply to anything" compliment—is that bad?)

Be grateful for the spouse God has given you on earth, and don't hesitate to express why.

66 : DON'T DITCH SINGLES

Don't ditch your single friends; that's what they dreaded when you got married. Many of them are still good friends to have, and so are you.

When you got married, your priorities changed, but that doesn't mean your friendships with singles have to disintegrate.

My husband and I have friends in all demographics. We believe it's a contiguous deal, relationally speaking. We give our single friends perspective on the future, and they keep us real and relational with people in every stage of life. We all stay well rounded.

PREGNANT, BABIES, AND CHILDREN IN YM

67: BETTER PARENT, BETTER VOLUNTEER

What a blessing that you are volunteering in YM as a parent! Thank you.

I have believed for years that being a parent makes someone a better youth worker and being a youth worker can make that person a better parent. That was certainly true for me.

Parenthood brings with it a certain humility you can't escape. And that's always a good thing to replicate in others.

Along with humility, the insight you gain as a parent will give you a greater appreciation and respect for other parents. If you were one of those nonparents who occasionally ranted,

"When I have kids, I'll never do that," you'll stop ranting soon enough. And that's a good thing for everyone.

68: YOUTH MINISTRY STARTS AT HOME

I remember a significant moment when my children were very young—one still in diapers. One day I sensed God drop this thought in my head—not an audible, booming voice, just a paternal nudge from my heavenly Father. And that thought went something like this: *You have a youth group, and you have two kids in it—your children.*

That divine pep talk came back to me more than once over the years. It was God's short and sweet encouragement to invest spiritually and emotionally first in my favorite future teenagers, before any other students.

That doesn't mean you should hide behind your children as an excuse not to serve in ministry. But neither should you overcommit.

Do what you can do enthusiastically, and give your family your best, not your leftovers.

As a personal motivator, fill in your children's names between these two statements:

I have a youth group at home, and I am its primary youth leader. The kids in my youth ministry are (write the name(s) of your child/children here):

With God's help, I will disciple my own children in a way that points them to Jesus.

(Bonus: Inspirational commitment statement to your children: *When you graduate into our youth ministry, if I'm still serving in it, I promise not to be the volunteer who puts the sock over the soda can and makes you drink from it. I will, however, be videotaping when you throw up. You're welcome.*)

VOLUNTEERING THROUGH THE AGES...ER, STAGES

69: THEY WON'T SPIT UP FOREVER

Build relationships with happy couples whose kids are older. Have them remind you that amid diapers, spit-up, and new floor decorations, you're not going crazy and you'll get through this season of life. Then ask them how. They probably have a couple of good tips.

When my children were babies, I stepped out of youth ministry altogether. As they became toddlers, I stepped back in but chose not to volunteer for multiple responsibilities. I had a sense of my personality and capacity, and felt I'd regret adding too much to my childrearing plate.

I remember a phone call with my mentor, expressing how different it was after years of being heavily involved. I missed volunteering in youth group. Knowing how ministry-committed I was, she said something that encouraged me and helped me never regret my priorities: "Danette, I know when you're changing those diapers, you may think, 'How is this impacting eternity?' But you'll never regret the time you spend with those babies."

My mentor's comments were a great reminder that babies don't spit up forever, and that toddlers don't keep throwing tantrums—at least, not the floor-in-the-store kind! They grow out of these stages eventually, and then it's on to another stage of life. So don't go crazy, don't give in, and don't miss the treasured moments. (Speaking of treasures, write down those cute things they say. Do this not only for sentimental reasons, but so that you'll have material for youth talks later on. It's a youth-worker parent's revenge!)

As our children grew in stages, Eric and I felt free to grow in responsibilities and commitments. Prioritizing family, work, and ministry was always a juggling act, and I had moments of being torn. But I never felt sorry that I gave my spouse and kids my best. I tried to give ministry my best as well, but if it came down to who got more of my best attitude, time, and heart, family always won.

VOLUNTEERING THROUGH THE AGES...ER, STAGES

You'll never regret that; neither will your family.

70: KEEP DATING!

See Thought 64. It's more costly but just as crucial now.

You need to continue connecting with each other. And don't only talk about your children. Talk about what God is doing in each of you, and what you need from each other. Keep laughing over the silly remarks you make at times. If it helps, bring your calendar along to make each other aware of youth ministry, family, and work events.

Confession: Sometimes Eric and I would save an argument for our date night. We were so busy that we didn't always have time for meaningful conversation, much less necessary conflict. And it wasn't usually a good idea to confront on the go. But over a relaxed dinner or dessert, our "intense fellowship" didn't take an ugly turn, simply because we were on our much-coveted date. We could hash and hammer things out but then move on. Most of the time.

71 : TO BRING OR NOT TO BRING THE KIDS

What about bringing kids to youth ministry events—to small group, youth group, retreats, and other activities and gatherings?

The answer depends on your church community dynamic—the size, the median age of volunteers, and, most importantly, the comfort level of both you and your leader in having children in a setting that requires your attention, leadership, or emotional and spiritual output.

Having the kids play in another room during your high school small group might provide little more than background noise. But hauling small children to a junior high retreat in the woods may leave you exhausted by the end because you couldn't leave them unsupervised and therefore couldn't really join in the retreat activities. If you have plenty of volunteers on hand, that may not be an issue. But if you're one of the few sponsors in tow, you may find your heart and focus frustrated by trying to prioritize two important parts of your life without shortchanging the other, especially if you're a single parent.

Aside from logistics, there are different ways to look at this, and a few of my youth ministry friends chimed in with their philosophies on this matter. No doubt, you'll find one or more resonating with you. Ultimately, take into consideration what's best for you, your family, and your youth ministry.

72: BRING 'EM

With healthy families in short supply in some areas, my friend Darren says, "Students need to see you with your kids." But he cautions, "It doesn't need to detract from the main purpose or distract you from the calling."

Janalynn and her husband, Shiloh, who are veteran volunteers, think it's best as a couple to work in ministry together as much as you can and involve your kids whenever possible. "For us, we feel it is important to have your children involved in ministry with you," she says. "It is hard when they are really little, but even then we took [our 6-year-old] with us to events and made it work. I want him to grow up seeing us serve in ministry where we have a passion and see what we are doing in ministry so that he can see that it is an important part of your walk with Christ. I also don't want him to feel resentful when we do spend a lot of time in ministry and he is not part of it—when he is there, he is involved and can see why we sacrifice our time and energy."

73: LEAVE 'EM

Junior high pastor Liz believes youth leaders should set boundaries when it comes to allowing children to accompany you to youth ministry shindigs. "Your own kids are always your primary ministry," she says. "Your ministry kids need to know they have your full attention at ministry times."

74 : FLIP A COIN ON 'EM

The deciding points on bringing your own kids to ministry events may vary. Flipping a coin probably won't cut it if it means leaving them home when you take your middle schoolers to a theme park, or towing your kids along on the whitewater rafting trip.

For Patti, it depends on three things:

1. Purpose—community emphasis vs. teaching emphasis.

2. Age appropriateness weighed against one's ability to participate fully with them present.

3. If other adults brought their own kids, would it bother me?

Though Janalynn feels strongly about including her young son in her ministry involvement, she will consider her own level of leadership for the particular event. "If Shiloh and I are both in charge of something," she said, "our son will stay home or go to Grandma's. The last few years we have brought him with us to the fall youth convention and he is definitely part of our small group. Both he and the kids enjoy this. However, if it is a training event and they offer child care, we would definitely use it." [14]

7 5 : WELCOME TO MY WORLD, PART 1

I never had to make the choice about bringing or leaving my kids when I attended youth ministry events. By the time I began volunteering again, Eric had stepped back from youth ministry and had become more involved in small groups and discipling young men. He supported my desire to work with teenagers and co-parented our children whether I was home or out. (He didn't *babysit*; that's what we paid nonrelatives to do when we went out on dates.)

From the time our kids were young, we took them on one-on-one dates to the library, the zoo, the park, or for a fast-food treat. Some years we were able to make it a weekly appointment; other seasons were sparse in money and overloaded in schedules. But for the most part, it's something our kids still demand—er, treasure. We're glad they even want to be seen with us (of course, if it's our treat, we may as well be a celebrity).

Anyway, before our kids were in our youth group but old enough to understand what I was doing as a volunteer, I began whetting their appetite for youth ministry. I did this by telling them stories about the fun activities, the silly games, and the skits. After returning from a weekend youth event, I liked to ask them, "As much fun as I had at the youth convention, if I had a choice between being with 900 fun and crazy teenagers and just you, which do you think I'd choose?" It didn't take too many times asking for them to say matter-of-factly, "Me!" So they understood that youth ministry was fun for me, but they still were my favorite kids.

I almost always I followed up with, "I can't wait for you to be in youth group with me!" This accomplished two things:

1. By the time they showed up for their first nights, they had a positive idea of what youth group would be like and looked forward to being there.

2. They understood that I wasn't infringing on their territory; I was allowing them to come into my world.

That second part is important. I've heard a number of parents say they'd like to volunteer in their youth ministry but their teenager, not the youth leader, won't let them. As I mentioned earlier, out of respect, I asked each of my children how they felt about me being a youth worker when they graduated into our youth ministry. For them, my role in youth ministry was normal, so when they started attending, it didn't dawn on them that I "shouldn't" be there.

Later on, I'll share some tips on how I navigated being a volunteer in my own kids' youth ministry. But I hope this section has given you some helpful ideas on what to do leading up to that.

TEENAGERS IN YM

76: "JUST WAIT UNTIL THEY'RE TEENAGERS!"

Parents enjoy saying to nonparents, "Wait until you have kids of your own." Parents of teenagers, now experts, get as much of a condescending kick out of telling parents of toddlers, "Just wait until they're teenagers!" Then what? You'll really understand? Your brain gets bigger? You want to yank out more of your hair? You'll stop judging other parents?

Those things are partly true. But by the time my oldest was in middle school, I'd volunteered for 19 years. From the time my children were born, I couldn't wait for them to become teenagers. Don't get me wrong; I enjoyed them through all age stages. But I had an especially joyful anticipation of my relationships with them as teenagers. I guess that's just how God wired me.

Now, you might be waiting for me to balance what I just wrote with either a reality-biting horror story or a fluffy rainbow version of parenting teenagers while in youth ministry.

I give you neither.

There were some frustrating moments that made me feel like I had no business working with anyone's teenagers, much less mine. There were times I liked other people's kids more than my own. They sure liked *me* more than my kids did at times!

But those resolve-challenging phases were part of parenting, whether in youth ministry or not. There was intense fellowship at the Matty Mansion over everything from attitudes to "forgotten" chores. Before our children were teenagers, I used to judge parents who made their teenagers stay home from youth group as punishment for delaying homework or violating a family rule. So dumb. "Why wouldn't you want them in the presence of God when they act up?" That very night they might have an encounter with God that hurtles them in repentance, falling before their parents in gurgling humility and gratitude!

And then I tripped into teenage land with my kids. For the most part, I enjoyed those years as much as I'd anticipated. But there were days I'd get so aggravated, and when those times happened to fall on youth group nights, lo and behold, I came *this* close to barking, "Li'l girl, if you don't straighten up right now, you'll stay home tonight!" I never pulled that trigger. But I finally understood how parents could get to that point. I quit judging.

Kids make choices about their attitudes and behavior. By the time they're teenagers, they have more control and awareness of cause and effect. We don't have to make as many excuses for them as we did when they were hungry, overly tired, need-my-comfort-item toddlers.

Still, the relationally beneficial things I'd looked forward to about having my own teenagers far outweighed the tough stuff. And those benefits refueled me as both a youth worker and a parent. If you don't believe me, just wait until you have teenagers!

77: WELCOME TO MY WORLD, PART 2

The next several thoughts contain ideas that originated in my head and appeared on YouthMinistry.com in an article called "How to Be Your Own Kid's Youth Leader." [15]

"Mom," my 13-year-old daughter announced with a straight face, "some of the kids in group really think you're cool." I bit my tongue and thought, "You're just now finding out?" For her first few years in youth group, Ariana liked me better as a youth worker than as a mom, so this was a revelation to her. The more other students told her what I meant to them (they didn't have to do chores at my house), the more respect she developed for me.

In the eyes of children, it seems like parents grow in stages. We go from Supersized Playmate to Superhuman Omniscient. We move from Unfair Dictator to Dumb, Palm Face Over-Reactor. If we keep communication, affection, and our hearts open with them, our teenagers' emotional pendulum may bring us back to something in between.

My husband and I got a surprise taste of the pendulum phenomenon during a drive with Denver, when he was 16. He was trying to draw in the car when he blurted, "Dad, use your magic dad powers to make the car fly."

Eric replied, "Oh, this road is rough."

"But you're Dad; you have super strength and you know everything."

I thought Eric might drive off the road.

I quipped, "It's taken 16 years for him to finally see you as you truly are."

Whether your teenagers see you as a super parent or super lame, the fun-maker or the fun-sucker, continue to be the mom or dad you need to be at home and the leader you need to be with other students. Eventually your offspring will see you for who you are: an individual.

78 : BEING YOUR OWN KIDS' YOUTH LEADER

A volunteer named Jeremy made an observation about parent youth workers. He said that youth group creates an environment where parents and their children can connect spiritually without any awkwardness, which is hard to re-create even at home. I agree, but both student and parent have to settle on some things.

When each of our children came of youth group age, I verbalized clear boundaries that may or may not fit your family. These policies didn't keep me from struggling, but they did keep me from over-competing between my dual roles of parent and youth worker. If you can, think and talk through them as a family before your kids begin their youth ministry journey.

79: MAKE AN OFFER YOUR TEENAGER CAN'T REFUSE

"I won't embarrass you in front of your friends if you don't embarrass me in front of mine." That was my No. 1 rule. "But if you disrespect me in front of other kids, all bets are off."

You may not have to go all *Godfather* on your kids, but this paid off in mutual respect with mine.

80: DON'T CREEP AT EVERY FUNCTION

I chose not to attend my kids' small groups. Only when Ariana asked to be in my high school girls' group was I her small group leader. Even then, I respected her opinions and individuality, and I didn't overtly mother her.

I went on most retreats and camps but stayed home from certain events. With both kids, I wanted them to attend functions where they could feel like separate individuals, without my eyes beading in on their every swig of soda.

81: DON'T CREEP DURING PRAYER TIME

When my kids responded to God during prayer times in our services, I didn't creep in on their vulnerability. On occasion I quietly asked permission to pray with them, but only when I sensed that would feel good to them as well. If they said no, I affirmed them and respected their verbal boundary. If they said yes, you can bet I prayed like I meant it. But I didn't "preach" a prayer to them or ask God for anything on their behalf that would embarrass them if another student overheard. ("Heavenly Father, as you know, Eric and I believe in arranged marriages, which I'm sure you'd agree never go out of fashion. I beseech you, gracious God, lay it on young Walfey Dittmueller Jr.'s heart to ask Mr. Matty to take out our daughter. Just sayin', O Lord.")

82: RISK ANALYSIS

I made a risky but important deal with my kids' key leaders—mind you, we're talking about people I trusted and knew had my back as a parent. One mom had done this with me years earlier when I was her daughter's youth leader.

I told those youth sponsors, "I want my child to feel free to share anything with you—even negative things about our relationship or their spiritual struggles. But they need to know that I'm not going to ask and you aren't going to tell me what they share."

My kids knew about this, I might add. There was always an open door but no unnecessary pressure to tell Eric and me everything. Risk analysis told us they would likely share things with other adults who weren't named "Mom" and "Dad." Rather than feel threatened by that, we fanned it with youth leaders for whom love and respect was mutual.

83: JUNIOR HIGHERS DON'T NEED HELP TO BOUNCE

A minor but practical rule I gave my kids in junior high: no caffeine at youth group. Have you observed middle schoolers who don't land after they start bouncing off the wall? My point exactly.

Once they were in high school, I stayed out of their snack-consumption business at church.

84: WHAT IF MY TEENAGER GETS HURT?

Even church kids can make thoughtless comments. We adults do it, too. But it's especially painful when you watch it happen to your children. There is a tightrope the parent youth worker must walk when another student says or does something that hurts your kid's feelings or bruises their ego.

Once, when Denver was in seventh grade, he posted something public on his Facebook wall about certain cartoon characters he liked. Sounds like a junior high guy to you and me, right? But a girl slightly older than him made a berating comment about how immature he was. One of his buddies added a joke that agreed with her assessment. It stung. My son pounded out an angry retort in all caps with lots of exclamation points.

For him, this was public humiliation and betrayal by his friends. I don't have to tell you that some friends may behave differently online than they would in real life. But I used it as an opportunity to teach him how to handle conflict, separate truths from lies in his own mind, and navigate hurt feelings with relational integrity. It was a painful but important conversation. He ended up deleting his public post and privately messaging both kids. The girl didn't care. The friendship with his buddy was salvaged.

Regardless of whether the offender is from church or school, how do you want your child to respond to personal offense? Your answer determines how you handle it, as both parent and leader.

Stay levelheaded and resist the urge to overreact in your defense of your son or daughter. Find out the whole story if your child wants to share it. Be as objective as you can in order to help your teenager gain an aerial view of the situation. The way you handle your kid's offense is important in shaping how he or she will respond.

85: WHAT IF MY TEENAGER GETS IN TROUBLE?

All his life, Denver has accepted almost anyone into his circle. He's highly relational and witty, so he draws a variety of friends to his side. I laughed to myself one night while watching a trio of guys who couldn't look and act more differently: my son, skater-emo image without the storm-cloud attitude; Jonny, crew-cut and athletic, an intimidatingly quiet gamer, headed into Army basic training that summer; and unrestrained Noah, red-plaid skinny jeans, dark eyeliner, and black nail polish. Watching these guys was the visual equivalent of playing dubstep, thrash metal, and punk rock music at the same time!

But back in his middle school days, my social dragonfly was an awkward spaz. Thankfully for me, he didn't make trouble for youth workers. He rarely disliked other students. But there were two in particular who managed to annoy him in elementary school, and there in junior high, they couldn't win for losing. I had confronted my young gun for kicking one kid in Sunday class and punching the other at camp.

I didn't begrudge Denver's feelings, but I made it clear that bad behavior wouldn't be tolerated in or outside of youth group. When our teenagers did stupid stuff at church by disrespecting people or property, I did my best to react with no lesser or greater intensity than if I were addressing bad behavior by another student.

86: GO FOR THE HEART, NOT THE JUGULAR

When either of our kids acted in less than angelic ways, I tried to refrain from playing the clergy card—as in, "Don't act up, because Daddy's a pastor and I'm a youth leader and you'll make us look bad."[16]

Years ago a girl whose parents were key leaders told me that she lived in a fishbowl because of their positions in the church. People were watching her life, her parents said, so she needed to make good choices on that basis. I get what they were teaching her, and of course I encouraged my kids to set good examples for others. But the pressure of the fishbowl means it can break more easily. My main message to my kids was, "Do what's right because you love God and you love us."

VOLUNTEERING THROUGH THE AGES...ER, STAGES

Despite how embarrassing our kids' public mistakes were, I always cared more about discipline shaping their hearts and making them wise than about how it made me look to other people.

87: WORTH IT

I've been honest about our flawed-but-fun family. We've had our share of stink—emotionally intense and draining times when one or more of us didn't like one or all of us. Through the years, we built in the sacrificial and sometimes desperate investments of time, relationship, and prayer. And I can honestly say I absolutely loved being my own kids' youth leader. (I asked them to read parts of this book and they agreed it was mutual — whew!)

When Ariana and Denver came into youth group, it was so fun to watch them play all these games I'd seen so many other kids play. Let's be honest: When it's your son or daughter, it's hilariously captivating. (Although I may or may not have pretended not to notice when my son threw up all the green candies in that one competition. And I may or may not have turned away gagging while another youth leader cleaned it up.)

How cool to be there when your own kids respond honestly to whatever the Holy Spirit is doing in the group. It doesn't matter whether you are the speaker or main facilitator of that moment. It's your kid. It only matters that you got to witness God at work in your child's life.

And what joy to catch your teenager serving or reaching out or doing anything wonderfully opposite of mouthing off, misbehaving, or "accidentally" clubbing a sibling with a plastic bat. (One of my children may or may not have done that and wondered why I got so mad over such a small amount of blood.)

If you can balance it just right, being a youth worker offers a window into a part of your child's life that you might not otherwise get.

VOLUNTEERING THROUGH THE AGES...ER, STAGES

It's kind of like Facebook—only in real life. And doing real life with your teenagers is worth it.

HEY! WHERE'D OUR KIDS GO? EMPTY-NEST YOUTH LEADERS

88: "NO, SERIOUSLY, HONEY, WHERE ARE THE KIDS?"

Remember the Toyota Sienna SE commercials featuring a hipster couple and their young kids? They rapped about parenting and rolling in their "swagger wagon," which made them obviously better than other parents. My favorite in the series is the signature music video, in which the balding father and cardigan-clad mother throw up gangster hands and ask to the beat, "Where my kids at? Where my kids at?" After asking several times, the music cuts, Dad turns to Mom and, in his suburban voice, asks, "No, seriously, honey, where are the kids?"[17]

Well, I'm about to ask that question. By the time this book goes to print, our kids will be both be in college—Denver starting and Ariana continuing that journey. I'm going to be bouncing through the house, "Where my kids at?"

Frankly, the empty nest is looking better and better to the Mister and me. We're super proud of both our children and will be thrilled to see them on school breaks and in the summer. But we're ready to have each other and the house all to ourselves.

For years, I wondered how I'd feel about working with teenagers after my own kids left. Would I remain passionate? Would I still give it my best without the ulterior motive of my own children's spiritual welfare at stake? Could I even connect with kids without a teenager in my house to keep me up on current music, fashion, and phrases?

I can't predict your journey. But because of my position when I was first hired at my current

VOLUNTEERING THROUGH THE AGES...ER, STAGES

church, I had a year without youth ministry involvement to test my heart. It didn't take that long to answer my questions. My love for teenagers and excitement to see God work in them is renewed every time I see the light bulb go on in their eyes during a small group discussion or a one-on-one conversation. I feel God's passion for their souls, and I know that God hasn't given up on their generation any more than God has given up on mine.

I asked several empty-nest volunteers questions about what keeps them volunteering in youth ministry even though they no longer have kids in the program (some never did), and what advantage they may have now as a youth mentor. Some respondents are from my church; others, from another state, answered anonymously. Reading the next several thoughts will encourage you if you're not there yet and affirm you if you are.

89: WHY STAY AFTER YOUR KIDS LEAVE?

- "Having a special place in my heart for youth that keeps me reaching out to them. It is a very challenging time of life for the students, and there is great need for adults to come alongside to help students negotiate the complexities of life. Those issues are becoming more complex all the time. I plan to continue in youth ministry until the Lord takes me in another direction." — Cindy

- "The main objective is to encourage youth to experience, learn about, and grow in Christ. This has nothing to do with whether or not my personal children are still involved in the youth program. I truly enjoy being with the youth, and they are way too important to ignore or forget about!" — Anonymous

- "I had been active as an adult Bible study teacher for many years and was comfortable in that arena. The idea of teaching youth was definitely out of my comfort zone because I wasn't sure I could relate well with them, something I still am working on. But I love this experience! The kids are so smart and their questions so challenging. I have learned many new ways to be an effective teacher, and I'm so happy in this arena. All God really needs is a willing spirit, and he supplies everything needed for the task. Thanks to my youth leader, Anne, for asking me to step out of my comfort zone." — Donna

- "Two things attracted me to working with young people. One was the statistical success of them 'getting it'—the rate of teens coming to Jesus at that age was significantly greater in these years. Also, seeing teens raised by single parents, who had no role models, no compass regarding morals or a Christian worldview. With each generation we earn our spots by availing ourselves through our time to gain understanding and influence to young lives. That hasn't changed—although

my effectiveness with each generation
is sometimes in question and gaining
understanding seems harder the greater
the gap in years. We empty nesters have
more time. Seems funny, but the less time
you have left to live, the more you see the
need to invest what you have." — Robin

90: IN WHAT WAYS ARE YOU BETTER AS A YOUTH LEADER NOW THAT YOU'RE AN EMPTY NESTER?

- "I don't feel like being an empty nester
  makes me any better, but I guess you have
  more experience to draw on. Actually,
  it can be a hindrance because when you
  had [kids in the home] they kept you up
  with the 'latest' in what was going on with
  youth and the world around them."
  — Anonymous

- "I think I love them even more and am
  more understanding. Yet still being an
  'outsider,' hopefully I can help them

without all the 'button-pushing' that a family relationship involves." — Anonymous

- "The youth in my group are the same age as my grandchildren. My grandkids are not in town, and I miss them a lot. Being with the youth fills a void. It gives me a chance to enjoy this time with them that I don't get with my own. At this stage in my life, I think I am able to just enjoy them more now that I am not trying to parent and teach youth their age. I care deeply about their concerns and what they value (or not), and I hope my comments and suggestions give them something to think about. I'm not one of their pals, but I hope they know that I love and accept them. I feel accepted by them, and that means a lot to me." — Donna

- "I have more time." — Anonymous

- "At my age I see myself as more intentional with the chances I get. I see some who are committed to friending young people, but are not as intentional about applying God's healing words to their world." — Robin

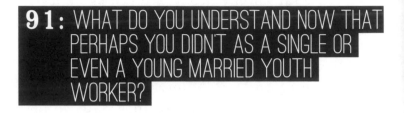

91: WHAT DO YOU UNDERSTAND NOW THAT PERHAPS YOU DIDN'T AS A SINGLE OR EVEN A YOUNG MARRIED YOUTH WORKER?

- "Every year of life gives you new opportunities for personal growth, and I've had lots of years to learn what works with youth and what doesn't. I have also seen huge changes in our culture over the years, which dramatically affect the lives of students. Our world challenges core beliefs and life philosophies, and it's crucial that students have good mentors to provide support, direction, and encouragement." — Cindy

- "The experiences learned from raising three boys are innumerable." — Anonymous

- "I'm 59. As I move from one phase of my life to another, I think I understand how little we understand about those who are older than us. No matter how hard we try to empathize, until we walk in those shoes, we can never understand fully. So we need to remember that about those younger than us." — Anonymous

- "I understand that our youth want to know God and how he fits with their values and lifestyle. They want to understand the connection because they are making important choices about what stays with them and what goes. Making sure our youth have a solid, biblical foundation to take with them into the world is one of the most important things youth leaders could ever do. Knowing that and being a part of that ministry is awesome to me." — Donna

- "When I am truly committed to loving others and seeing from their perspective, then I can gain understanding. Some of the hardest young people seem to melt when they can feel your love and acceptance without prejudice. I am a recovering 'Piercing Pharisee.' I have seen many times that I could not see past the nose ring to see the eyes crying out for God's love. Funny thing is, each generation has a greater shock factor as far as fads go. I still tell kids who wear their britches down around their knees to pull them up, but now I tell them with a smile." — Robin

9 2 : FINAL OBSERVATIONS FROM LEADING AT THIS STAGE OF LIFE

- "The energy-level gap is definitely widening, along with the technical-knowledge gap. I'm very likely to ask the youth for help with nearly anything that's somehow connected to a computer or cell phone. I think my patience is improving. It also takes quite a bit to surprise me. I can anticipate most of what they're thinking and about to do. It's good for me as well! I learn something from the youth on a daily basis." — Anonymous

- "Certainly, the perspective of an old guy that has been through what the kids are facing in their future is a benefit. But what I find most is that at this stage of life what the kids bring to the table keeps the old guy young and constantly learning from them." — Anonymous

- "I see more parents wanting to be friends...they are parents first. [As a dad,] I ran as a buffer to outside influences. It wasn't always popular, but it was effective. I get confused by high schoolers trading in their youth group 'membership card' for a [fast food] uniform. Just when young people need that relationship [with Jesus] solidified and nurtured, they are allowed to trade it in for a job at $6.65 per hour." — Robin

CHAPTER 7

FULL CIRCLE: LEADERSHIP DEVELOPMENT AND SPIRITUAL MATURITY

YOUR YOUTH MINISTRY STORY CONTINUES

As long as you say yes, God will use you in the ministry and use the ministry in you. The transformation flows both directions.

9 3 : YOUTH MINISTRY REPLACING GOD?

I have a couple of tough questions that are worth asking ourselves now and then throughout our youth ministry journey: Am I so good at youth ministry and fulfilled in my role that it could easily replace my relationship with God? At this moment, do I love what God is doing in my youth ministry more than I love God?

Remember that even a shepherd needs a break from the sheep. Knowing that God has his eye on us first is good motivation to keep our eyes on God—first.

Is there a balance? In some ways, it seems there will always be conflicting messages in ministry. One says, "You can never do enough! Don't just stand there; do something!" The other mental memo reads, "You can't earn

God's favor by works—that's legalism. Don't just do something; stand there!"

The tension between these two can be confusing and frustrating. We have to know exactly what God has called us to do. It would be easy for leaders to condescend about small ministries, as though there were differences in the quality of blood, sweat, and tears poured out over fewer students. And I've heard leaders of small ministries make subtle comments about big ministries, insinuating (as some poor do of the rich), that there was no God-breathed effort to grow that beast. *Surely it's 90 percent hype or show.*

Last time I checked, big ministries didn't just sprout up out of the ground without planting and watering. The late Christian businessman Jim Rohn wrote that the greatest form of maturity is at harvest time: "This is when we must learn how to reap without complaint if the amounts are small and how to reap without apology if the amounts are big." [18]

By now I hope you realize (perhaps for the thousandth time) that God smiles on you for what you do for *him*, small or big. What God really wants for you is a shepherd's heart, like his Son. God will multiply your rewards in time.

So keep God in his proper place and youth ministry in its place. As long as you honestly do it for God, he's still smiling.

For every disciplined effort, there are multiple rewards. That's one of life's great arrangements. —Jim Rohn[19]

94: RAISE YOUR R.Q. WITH STUDENTS

Raise what I call your R.Q.—Relational Quotient—by spending some time with the tough kids, those who really need the one-on-one attention and may challenge you. But also build relationships with teenagers who are easy to spend time with, who fuel and don't drain you.

95: RAISE YOUR R.Q. WITH ADULTS

Along the same lines, make sure you're getting time with three types of adults:

1. Those you are investing in

2. Iron-sharpens-iron friends, with whom you can do life on a mutually beneficial growth path

3. People you respect, from whom you want to learn

Too much time with any one of these types doesn't provide a well-balanced diet of relational, spiritual, and intellectual nutrition.

Who, in your life, raises your R.Q in any of these three ways? Write down their names:

The next few thoughts contain ideas that originated in my head and appeared on YouthMinistry.com in an article called "Boundaries: Which ABCs Do You Recite When You're Vulnerable?"[20]

96: WHEN IT COMES TO SIN, THERE'S NO SUCH THING AS DAMAGE CONTROL

"One night at youth group, I'd responded to the youth pastor's message, crying and praying to God over my insecurities and sins. Later, spotting me in the near-empty parking lot, the youth pastor motioned for me to sit in their vehicle before I went home. The youth pastor had seen me crying and asked why. Trying to be rational, I pointed to a passenger sitting in my car, waiting for a ride home. I told the youth pastor, 'I know I can tell you anything, but I've been crying. Let's talk another time when I'm not so emotional.' My youth pastor didn't let it go. I was, after all, one of the youth sponsors, and a good youth pastor looks after leaders. The youth *pastor looked me in the eye and said in a soft, sincere voice, 'They can wait. Talk to me.' We ended up talking longer and saying more than we intended. Simply put, that's the night I gave my youth pastor my heart."*

Variations of that story, as told by a volunteer youth worker, have been repeated far too many times. The details vary: gender of youth leaders, and whether the involvement is between two leaders, a leader and a student, or a leader and someone entirely unassociated with the church. Regardless of variation, this scenario, if taken any further, is devastating to everyone involved. And the fallout that bleeds over to others is neither predictable nor controllable. When we sin, damage control goes out the window.

97 : KNOW YOURSELF. HELP YOURSELF

Kara Powell, a youth ministry professor at Azusa Pacific University, talks about "emotional affairs" in youth ministry[21] (two decades ago Jeanne Mayo called it "emotional adultery"). "You're sharing the experience of lives being changed, you're excited about what God's doing, and you're passionate about your work. It's easy to let that passion spill over into unhealthy relationships with opposite sex volunteers or paid coworkers." Powell says it may not by physical, "but you're flirting with an equally explosive form of intimacy."

The volunteer in Thought 96 was caught in a moment of vulnerability. Without spiritual and relational guardrails—such as consistent time alone with God, Scripture study, healthy boundaries in relationships, and accountability—all of us are vulnerable.

The result may not be an emotionally or sexually inappropriate relationship. Vulnerability could invite unhealthy coping involving food, money, media, money, or escapism. Pick your poison; even amoral indulgences can become too much of a good thing when you're not getting your legitimate needs met in appropriate ways.

Know yourself. Help yourself. Keep yourself close to God.

98: AS YOU ARE IN CHURCH, SO BE IN THE WORKPLACE

One of the students in our youth ministry confessed to me that he was disillusioned by his boss. "He's almost always in a bad mood. He's really nice to potential customers. But with service and delivery people, he acts like a jerk." After he gave me a few examples, I saw what this kid meant.

The painful part of this story—and the source of my young friend's disillusionment—is that his boss was also a volunteer in our youth ministry: a super nice guy, always ready with a pat on the back and a witty one-liner. I had no reason to doubt his salvation. Bad moods and rudeness aren't centric to salvation. But I don't have to tell you how damaging double-messages coming from our lives are.

In our leadership development program for emerging adults, Christ's Place Leadership College, I tell our students to remember the first name in that title: Christ. "You represent Christ first. Act in a way that reflects and honors him."

Secondly, because our church happens to be called Christ's Place, they represent our church. "You never know when you're out and about—filling up at the gas station, out to eat with friends, or buying groceries—who may show up to our church and remember the way you treated them, how you tipped them, and the vibe you gave off."

So behave in such a way that you won't be embarrassed either when you see that person again, or when you see Jesus one day.

99: REASONS WHY I DO THIS

I don't remember who gave me this idea, but years ago I began keeping a file of meaningful cards and notes from students, youth leaders, and parents. Now and then, on hard days, I read some of them. Yes, it's self-serving. It's also very encouraging to be reminded that teenagers are worth the investment.

Think of every game, concert, recital, tournament, and play you've shown up for.

Every tough conversation you have that results in repentance, reconciliation, and a stronger relationship.

Every late-night time of cleaning up after everyone else has left.

Every dollar you've given to help a student get to the retreat.

Every time you took a chewing out by a parent without biting back.

Is it worth it?

Some days we can't answer that question easily. We may say, "Of course," and mean it. But on any given day you and I could be feeling the sting of conflict, the heartache of kids who make painfully consequential choices or walk away from Jesus.

The voice in our head whispers like an emotional assassin and says things like:

"What are you doing here? You could use your time in better ways."

"You're not appreciated. Do something else."

"Who do you think you are? You don't have what it takes to make a difference."

And the worst: "You're a failure at this. Why don't you quit?"

The answer: Teenagers are worth it. Jesus is worth it.

Here are some notes from teenagers to remind you of what you're doing—that youth ministry is a great use of time, that you make a difference, and that even on the toughest days, you shouldn't quit.

Dear Volunteer,

I know I don't give you back what you give me. I don't always act like I'm listening. When certain friends are around, I don't even act like I see you. And I don't always respond to God when you challenge me to.

But don't think I'm ungrateful for what you give me...noticing me when I show up, asking me how I'm doing even when I hardly talk, the texts to let me know you're praying for me in the toughest class, and the money to buy a snack at the retreat.

Please don't stop challenging me to walk with God. I really want to. But it's hard sometimes. I feel pulled so hard in both directions— toward God and toward the world. And the voices in the world are loud and many and constant. I really need your voice to continue to be consistent.

I don't say it because I'm insecure, and it doesn't usually dawn on me that you need to hear it. But...

FULL CIRCLE

...thank you.

—The teenager in your youth group you think doesn't get anything out of it

Dear Volunteer,

Thanks for praying for me. You're all spiritual so that's probably the easiest part of your non-job. Thanks also for encouraging me to have a better relationship with my parents and for telling me how "it counts at home." That's probably the hard part, saying things you know teenagers might not want to hear.

I really had some hard times at home and wasn't getting along with my parents very well. What you said changed my attitude at home and made me realize that it really does count at home.

Thank you.

Dear Volunteer,

You cannot fathom how a person can be impacted by such little things like noticing a young boy for just a moment in life and how that has influenced his future up to today.

I know I was a mouthy spaz in middle school who turned into a come-and-go flake in high school. But I listened more than you thought and applied more than you saw.

I finally graduated from college and have been on my job for almost a year. I got plugged in at a good church (you were always harping on that to the seniors!) and guess what? I just started volunteering in the youth group. Crazy, huh?

You cannot and will not ever know how just a moment that you chose to give me week after week—noticing me, being cool with my friends, asking me questions, and getting in my face at times—impacted my life.

Now it's my turn to give some teenagers a few moments. Thanks for showing me how.

FULL CIRCLE

Dear Volunteer,

What can I say? You have always helped me when I was havin' a hard time and increased my faith in Jesus. Who knows what path I would be on if you weren't there to guide me through! Your hospitality and kindness has meant a great deal to me during this year! I (heart) u!

Your student

— An actual note I received, written inside a Napoleon Dynamite card

ENDNOTES

1. I wish I had a nickel for every time between 1985 and 1989 that I heard Jeanne make this kind of statement in a leadership meeting, from the stage, or over coffee. I could buy a lifetime supply of the hair color I apply every month.

2. Another nugget of wisdom received personally from Jeanne Mayo.

3. I highly recommend the book *Boundaries* by Dr. Henry Cloud and Dr. John Townsend (Zondervan 1992).

4. *Good to Great: Why Some Companies Make the Leap and Others Don't* (Jim Collins, HarperCollins Publishers Inc., New York, 2001) is a book worth reading for top-tier leaders of teams in either ministry or the marketplace.

5. Some of my favorite free sites include thesource4ym. com, egadideas.com, morethandodgeball.com, and the freebies section of youthministry.com.

6. This is my all-time favorite YM conference. Not your typical seminar experience, SYMC (youthministry. com/symc) is Jesus-centered, extremely practical, and spiritually and emotionally refueling.

7. Nathaniel Yaekel, "Portrait of a Musher," Point Press, Vol. 2, Issue 1, Jan. 5, 2002; 4pointspress.com/presspoints/2002/0105/travel_ntips.html

8. Sources for information in this thought include Lance Mackey's Comeback Kennel (mackeyscomebackkennel.com/ContactUs.html) and Wikipedia (en.wikipedia.org/wiki/Mushing).

9. Donald O. Clifton and Edward "Chip" Anderson, with Laurie A. Schreiner, *StrengthsQuest: Discover and Develop Your Strengths in Academics, Career, and Beyond* (Washington, DC: Gallup Press, 2006).

10. Christ's Place Leadership College (cplace.org/cplc) is a nine-month leadership development program for high school graduates and young adults who want to refine their leadership skills in a structured, healthy environment with seasoned leaders, whether their calling is to ministry or the marketplace.

11. Rod Whitlock first shared his thoughts about the shepherd vs. the hired hand with me in a telephone interview. I used many of these thoughts in an article of the same title for the September/October 2009 issue of Youthworker Journal. You can read the entire article, "The Shepherd vs. the Hired Hand," online: youthspecialties.com/articles/the-shepherd-vs.-the-hired-hand.

12. allaboutsheepdogs.com

13. answers.yahoo.com/question/index?qid=20090323180932AAFURCH

14. *Two Sides: Finding What Fits Your Youth Ministry* from Simply Youth Ministry includes a helpful section

on "My Kids" that provides additional insights and opinions on this matter to help you think through these kinds of decisions.

15. youthministry.com/articles/families/how-be-your-own-kid's-youth-leader. Original copyright 2011, YouthMinistry.com, all rights reserved. Used with permission.

16. After we went into full-time ministry, one of my rules for my children was that they couldn't play the PK card—as in, "I can do this or that because I'm a pastor's kid." Nor could they use it as an excuse for certain attitudes or behaviors. If they ever tried, they got the stink eye from yours truly. And trust me, you *don't* want to get the stink eye from The Momness.

17. Toyota Swagger Wagon Campaign — toyotaswaggerwagon.com

18. jimrohn.com/index.php?main_page=page&id=704

19. jimrohn.com/index.php?main_page=page&id=1288

20. www.simplyyouthministry.com/from-the-field 185.html

21. This is a tremendous and straightforward article about the "pink flags" of relational youth ministry. "Mars and Venus: Men and Women Together in Ministry" by Kara Powell, posted on October 9, 2009, Youth Specialties Article Archives (youthspecialties. com/articles/mars-and-venus-men-and-women-together-in-ministry).